Leslie Marmon Silko

Twayne's United States Authors Series

Frank Day, Editor
Clemson University

TUSAS 692

LESLIE MARMON SILKO
Photo by Lee Marmon, Silko's father.

Leslie Marmon Silko

Gregory Salyer

Huntingdon College

Twayne Publishers
An Imprint of Simon & Schuster Macmillan
New York

Prentice Hall International
London • Mexico City • New Delhi • Singapore • Sydney • Toronto

Twayne's United States Authors Series No. 692

Leslie Marmon Silko
Gregory Salyer

Twayne Publishers
An Imprint of Simon & Schuster Macmillan
1633 Broadway
New York, NY 10019

Library of Congress Cataloging-in-Publication Data

Salyer, Gregory.
   Leslie Marmon Silko / Gregory Salyer.
      p.   cm. — (Twayne's United States authors series ; TUSAS 692)
   Includes bibliographical references and index.
   ISBN 0-8057-1624-6 (alk. paper)
      1. Silko, Leslie, 1948–   —Criticism and interpretation.
   2. Women and literature—United States—History—20th century.
   3. Laguna Indians in literature.   I. Title.   II. Series.
   PS3569.I44Z87   1997
   813'.54—dc21   97-37697
                                                        CIP

10 9 8 7 6 5 4 3 2 1

Printed in the United States of America

For Robert Detweiler
Scholar, Mentor, and Friend

Contents

Preface

I remember the first time I saw Leslie Marmon Silko's novel *Ceremony*. I was a graduate student at Emory University, and, while passing by a display of ethnic women writers in the campus bookstore, I was drawn to the striking cover of Fritz Scholder's "Unfinished Crow," which appears on the earlier Penguin editions of the novel. After reading the comments on the back, I purchased it and made a mental note to add this book to the growing list of those I needed to read to further my education. It was some time before I finally sat down and read the opening lines: "Ts'its'tsi'nako, Thought-Woman, / is sitting in her room / and whatever she thinks about / appears." I was confused from page one. What was this poem, and why begin a novel this way? Why all the white space, sometimes almost a full page, between lines? As I read on, my confusion deepened to the point where I put the book down and did not pick it up again for awhile. I did this three times before I finally finished *Ceremony*, and when I did finish it, I was unsure of what I had just read. In spite of my ignorance and naïveté, I knew that the appearance of this novel was itself an event of great importance. Something was happening in those pages that could be glimpsed only faintly through the lenses of my academic training to that point. My initial response was more right than I had thought. This book was going to educate me in ways that I had not imagined.

Since those painful and enlightening first moments with *Ceremony*, I have taught it, read papers about it, and now am writing about it myself. I bring to this endeavor conflicting thoughts and emotions. First of all, I know that there is still much to learn from Silko's work. Like any great author, Silko challenges, informs, disturbs, and edifies me every time I encounter her. Her stories are not bedtime stories, although they have the flavor of myth and magic. She presents American culture in all of its nightmares, yet she does not eradicate the possibility of miracles and healing. Her criticisms of political and social ideologies of oppression and racism are devastating, and yet she imagines a future in which all who love and respect creation will survive and thrive. I want readers of this book to experience Silko's power and grace in a way that is as undiluted as possible. At the same time, there are things readers can know that will enhance their reading without mitigating the effect of meeting Silko face-to-face on the page. To miss the importance of Yellow Woman to Pueblo mythology and to Silko herself is to miss a great deal in reading any of her works. Likewise, understanding Silko's desire to continue in print the oral traditions of her ancestors offers readers a more complete experience of the stories. It is that razor's edge between being helpful and intrusive that I endeavor to walk in this book. These are after all Silko's stories. Ultimately, I am only retelling them. While I certainly do not want to present myself as a storyteller, I do realize that this book, by virtue of being a bridge between Silko and other readers, is a continuation of the story. With that comes a heavy responsibility. As Ku'oosh says to Tayo in *Ceremony:* "That was the responsibility that went with being human . . . the story behind each word must be told so there could be no mistake in the meaning of what had been said; and this demanded great patience and love" (35–36). It is with such love and patience that I undertake to retell the tales of a master storyteller in the form of a critical introduction to her work.

Much of Silko's writing overflows traditional categories of criticism and does not lend itself to familiar interpretive strategies. Expectations of nonnative readers are likely to be overturned, and Silko explores profound themes such as language, identity, and history from a distinctly Native American point of view. In the chapters that follow, I attempt to illuminate the experience of reading Silko diachronically since that experience is vital to understanding the stories. I also offer a synchronic analysis of themes in her stories in light of her Laguna heritage and her desire to continue the oral tradition in print. The former approach examines the subtlety of the works in a microscopic fashion, whereas the latter uses a telescopic view to explore the breadth of the themes. The chapters incorporate these two goals explicitly or implicitly, so for the poetry and fiction (*Laguna Woman, Ceremony, Storyteller,* and *Almanac of the Dead*) there are sections of the chapters that deal explicitly with the reading experience, while for the other books this approach is blended with an interpretation of the various themes found there. My larger goal is to provide all readers with a sense of the subtlety and scope of Silko's body of work. The final chapter offers an assessment of Silko's place in American literature and discusses the cultural work that her writing performs.

In the summer of 1995, I had the great privilege to study at Yale University in a summer seminar sponsored by the National Endowment for the Humanities. In addition to reading for the seminar, which was on the Bible and literature, I was doing research for a paper on the use of the Bible in Native American literature and collecting articles on Leslie Marmon Silko in preparation for writing this book. I was so involved with these tasks that I was not able to visit the Beinecke Rare Book Library on Yale's campus until my last week there. Two former students were visiting me that week, and they suggested that we go into the Beinecke to see a Gutenberg Bible, among other things. I was entranced by the collection, which was carefully displayed behind glass walls and cases. I finally made my way over to the east end of the library where I was treated to a vision of a Gutenberg Bible. One of only 22 in existence, it almost shimmered in the subdued light of the Beinecke. Here was the invention that was supposed to end storytelling as it was known. Turning to my left, I examined the adjacent display case, where I stood for some time as my mind processed what I was seeing. In this case was a typescript with much scribbling in the marginalia in at least two different colors of ink. It was the original manuscript of Leslie Marmon Silko's first novel, *Ceremony*. I can think of no better illustration of the importance of Silko's work. The juxtaposition of a book about the power of stories and the primary character in the story of the book displayed a powerful convergence of history and culture, and from that convergence a simple fact emerged: The story never ends.

Acknowledgments

I am very grateful for the support of Huntingdon College and President Wanda Bigham during the writing of this book. Dean William F. Pollard, vice-president for academic affairs and Professor Frank Buckner, chair of the Division of Humanities, provided a course reduction and encouragement that were invaluable to me. Nordis Smith of the Houghton Memorial Library searched far and wide to obtain articles and other sources crucial to the research for this book. Many other people helped in a variety of ways, including Nancy Jackson at the Huntingdon College bookstore and a number of people who have spoken to me after lectures or papers. A summer seminar sponsored by the National Endowment for the Humanities at Yale University led by Michael Holquist and Walter Reed provided access to the Sterling Memorial Library's vast holdings and also allowed me to participate in edifying conversations about Native American literature, the Bible, and Mikhail Bakhtin. Sandra Sprayberry of Birmingham-Southern College read portions of the manuscript and offered helpful suggestions. Lee Marmon (Silko's father) offered southwestern hospitality during my visits to the Blue-Eyed Indian Bookstore in Casa Blanca. He also allowed me to wander around the Marmon ranch near Acoma, which is the setting for much of *Ceremony*. Through his generosity I was able to follow in Tayo's footsteps, as it were, and experience firsthand the power and beauty of the land that shaped his daughter's imagination and identity. Leslie Marmon Silko herself was kind and forthcoming with answers to my questions in spite of the fact that she was immersed in her newest novel, *Garden in the Dunes*. Finally, I would like to thank the students of Huntingdon College for being interested in what interests me and for allowing me to learn with them.

Chronology

1948   Leslie Marmon Silko born 5 March to Leland (Lee) Howard Marmon and Mary Virginia Leslie in Albuquerque, New Mexico. Grows up in Laguna, New Mexico, about 50 miles west of Albuquerque

1958   Attends Manzano Day School, a Catholic school in Albuquerque

1964   Attends the University of New Mexico

1966   Marries Richard C. Chapman

        Robert William Chapman born

1969   B.A. in English, University of New Mexico

        Begins law school at the University of New Mexico in the American Indian Law School Fellowship Program

        Separates from and eventually divorces Richard Chapman

        Publishes first story, "The Man to Send Rain Clouds," in *New Mexico Quarterly*

1971   Leaves law school, returns to the University of New Mexico to take graduate English courses

        Leaves the university to teach on the Navajo reservation at Tsaile

        Awarded an NEA Discover Grant

        Marries John Silko (they later divorce)

1972   Cazimir Silko born

1973   Moves to Ketchikan, Alaska, and begins writing *Ceremony*

1974   Publishes several stories, including the title story, in *The Man to Send Rain Clouds*

        Laguna Woman: Poems

        Wins poetry award from *The Chicago Review*

1975   "Lullaby" selected as one of the twenty best short stories of 1975

Meets poet James Wright at a writing conference

1976   Returns to Laguna

A one-act play of "Lullaby," adapted with Frank Chin, is first performed

1977   Wins Pushcart Prize for Poetry

Ceremony

1978   Moves to Tucson, begins teaching at the University of Arizona

Begins correspondence with James Wright that becomes *The Delicacy and Strength of Lace*

1980   James Wright dies of cancer

Film: *Estoyehmuut and the Gunnadeyah* [Arrowboy and the Destroyers]

1981   *Storyteller*

Recipient of MacArthur Prize Fellowship

1982   Videotape: *Running on the Edge of the Rainbow: Laguna Stories and Poems*

1986   *The Delicacy and Strength of Lace: Letters,* edited by Anne Wright

Wins *Boston Globe* prize for nonfiction

1988   Wins New Mexico Endowment for the Humanities "Living Cultural Treasure" Award

1989   Wins University of New Mexico's Distinguished Alumnus Award

1991   *Almanac of the Dead*

Wins Lilla Wallace *Reader's Digest* Fund Writers Award

1993   *Sacred Water: Narratives and Pictures*

1996   *Yellow Woman and a Beauty of the Spirit: Essays on Native American Life Today*

1997   *Garden in the Dunes*

Chapter One

Leslie Marmon Silko:
The Story of a Storyteller

It is somewhat ironic to begin a book on Leslie Marmon Silko with a biographical sketch. After all, Silko's work, more than that of other writers, is autobiographical through and through. Her 1981 collection of short stories, poems, tales, and photographs titled *Storyteller* is sometimes called an autobiography, and for good reason. It begins with her memory of a tall Hopi basket full of her father's photographs, which evoke a narration that connects her ancestors, both recent and remote, to time and land. Throughout the book we are privy to the Laguna gossip and mythology that helped to shape Silko's identity. *Storyteller* also illustrates the nature of storytelling in Laguna; namely, it finds its genesis in landscape and community rather than in individual creation. Silko has no story that she calls her own, but she considers herself to be the product of land, time, and language. In a 1976 interview she explains: "In a sense you are told who you are, or you know who you are by the stories that are told about you. I see now that the ideas and dreams and fears and wonderful and terrible things that I expected might happen around the river were just part of an identity that the stories had made for it. By going to the river, I was stepping into that identity."[1]

Interestingly, Silko does not consider herself a storyteller in the traditional sense because she believes that she lacks the requisite ability to give spontaneous presentations that play off other stories. In other words, she is a writer, someone who likes to think through implications and dynamics to enhance and augment her articulation of a story. There is, however, a larger sense of storytelling than the performative one; for Silko, storytelling is more akin to a worldview. In an interview with Kim Barnes, Silko notes: "When I say 'storytelling,' I don't just mean sitting down and telling a once-upon-a-time kind of story. I mean a whole way of seeing yourself, the people around you, your life, the place of life in the bigger context, not just in terms of nature and location, but in terms of what has gone on before, what's happened to other people."[2] For Silko, then, stories are her identity, her biography.

Leslie Marmon Silko was born March 5, 1948 to Leland (Lee) Howard Marmon and Mary Virginia Leslie in Albuquerque, New Mexico. She grew up in Laguna with her extended family, including a great-grandmother, several uncles and aunts, and other relatives. Silko derives great significance from her mixed ancestry: "My family are the Marmons at Old Laguna on the Laguna Pueblo Reservation where I grew up. We are mixed bloods—Laguna, Mexican, and white—but the way we live is like Marmons, and if you are from Laguna Pueblo you will understand what I mean. All those languages, all those ways of living are combined, and live somewhere on the fringes of all three. But I don't apologize for this any more—not to whites, not to full bloods—our origin is unlike any other. My poetry, my storytelling rise out of this source."[3] From the biographical note to *Laguna Woman,* we read: "I suppose at the core of my writing is the attempt to identify what it is to be a half-breed or mixed-blooded person; what it is to grow up neither white nor full traditional Indian."[4] Issues of boundary and identity continue to permeate Silko's writing.

Silko attended Laguna Day School, an Indian boarding school, until the fifth grade, where she was prohibited from using the Keresan language that her grandmothers and aunts employed in their storytelling. Eventually she was taken to a Catholic day school in Albuquerque—a 100-mile round-trip—where she finished out her school years. By age 8 she had her own horse and could herd cattle at the Marmon ranch. By 13 she was hunting deer with her family and even had her own rifle. Her childhood experiences were a blend of remarkable inclusivity and stark differences. She has said in interviews that her Laguna upbringing was a kind of sheltering experience, where the comforting influences of her extended family provided a standard by which to measure the lives of her white friends. For example, she rarely felt the sexism that permeates American culture because in Laguna—a matriarchal and matrilineal society—women plastered houses, owned property, and ran the communities while men did the weaving and basket making and much of the child rearing. Her grandmother Lillie was a Model A mechanic and worked in the family laundry lifting and repairing machines until she was in her nineties. Silko's aunt Susie, a graduate of Carlisle Indian School and Dickinson College, came back to Laguna to teach in the 1920s. Silko remembers her reading at the kitchen table with books and papers spread out over the oilcloth. "She had come to believe very much in books and in schooling," writes Silko in *Storyteller,* and "she was a brilliant woman, a scholar of her own making who has cherished the

Laguna stories all her life" (4, 7). The influence these women had upon Silko is revealed in the smooth brilliance she employs when writing about women and identity.

It would be incorrect, however, to paint Silko's childhood as a kind of utopian existence. While she was wrapped warmly in the company of family and stories, there were numerous times when her identity clashed with the dominant culture's values. In the Bureau of Indian Affairs day school that she attended in Laguna, she experienced what it meant to be a mixed-blood. Tourists driving Old Route 66 would often stop by the school to photograph "real Indians." She remembers being in the first grade and posing for one such picture. Just as the white tourist was about to snap the photograph, he looked at Leslie Marmon and said, "Not you," and motioned for her to move away from her classmates. Her embarrassment was so deep that she recalls it to this day. She writes that her classmates were simply confused, but she knew what was happening. She had been singled out because she was part white.[5]

Further friction between Laguna and white expectations occurred when she was in the sixth grade. In the author's note to *Sacred Water,* she recalls her difficulties in moving to the Catholic school in Albuquerque and her desire to fit in with her new classmates. Apparently, a dirty joke had been going around the school despite (or because of) the fact that students telling it would most certainly be reprimanded. Silko, an obviously precocious 11-year-old, decided to "publish" the joke in a magazine that she would edit and print. She titled her magazine *Nasty Asty,* decorated the pages with silhouettes and bunny tales and ears cut from her father's *Playboy* magazines, and hand-printed two copies of it for distribution to the class. She says that she considered cutting out pictures of bare breasts to adorn the magazine but knew even then that "color magazine photographs of bare breasts would over-power and take too much attention away from the text."[6] She notes that at Laguna her mother often joked about the images in Playboy; therefore, she knew not to take the magazine too seriously, certainly not as seriously as *Nasty Asty.* Silko worked far into the night to produce two copies of her magazine, which was well received in the Catholic day school's sixth-grade class. Of course, she was called into the principal's office eventually, but she was saved from expulsion by the loyalty of the class, who maintained that the young Leslie Marmon's only crime was writing down what had already been circulating orally. Silko admits that this incident foreshadowed her future negotiations of the boundaries laid down by the dominant culture, where "the written word carries far more weight and authority than the spoken word." Silko essentially repeated her sixth-grade experience when she wrote, photographed, designed, sewed, and glued the first copies of *Sacred Water*. She writes that "the hand-made copies of *Sacred Water* look as if a fifth-grade child sewed and glued them; and indeed, while I am sewing and gluing the books, I feel magically transported back to the blissful consciousness of a fifth grader" (*SW*, 80).

Leslie Marmon would continue to pursue her interest in words and images throughout her life. She attended the University of New Mexico, where she received a B.A. degree in English in 1969. During this time she married Richard Chapman and had her first son, Robert. The same year she graduated, she published her first story, which provided the title for an important collection of Native American writing, *The Man to Send Rain Clouds*. This piece was generated in 1967 during a creative writing course in which she was required to write a short story. Silko had read in the Laguna paper about a local priest who was upset that he had not been called to officiate at the traditional Laguna burial of an old man at a sheep camp. The Silko simply retold this story, focusing on the setting and the emotions of the participants. It came easy for her, and from then on she knew she was a writer.

Despite the fact that she was published while in college, Silko did not initially see writing as a vocation. After graduating from college, her next move was to enroll in the University of New Mexico Law School through a program designed to help Native Americans represent themselves in legal disputes. She had thought since high school that she would be able to bring justice to her people through the American legal system. As tribal treasurer, her father had filed land claims against the state of New Mexico, attempting to reclaim six million acres granted to the Pueblo people by the king of Spain. She recalls: "The lawyer hired by the Pueblo of Laguna and the expert witnesses, archaeologists, used to meet at our house to prepare to testify in court" (*YWBS*, 18). She completed three semesters of her program before concluding that injustice is endemic to American jurisprudence. The turning point for her was when her class read an appeal to the U.S. Supreme Court to halt the execution of a black man convicted of strangling a white librarian in Washington, D.C. The execution order was upheld in spite of the fact that the convicted man was retarded and had no understanding of his crime. Silko remarks: "That case was the breaking point for me. I wanted nothing to do with such a barbaric legal system" (*YWBS*, 20). She decided that the only way to seek justice was through the power of storytelling.

After law school, Silko returned to Albuquerque to take graduate courses in English at her alma mater. While enrolled in a course on William Blake that explored the relationship between visual images and the written text, she also took a beginning photography class. As a child, Silko had spent many hours watching her father, Lee—a professional photographer—work in his darkroom. The photography class inspired her to tell a story that would incorporate photographs with written narrative. She became disillusioned with the Blake class and dropped out of it and eventually out of graduate school. Her interest in the visual and the written would be expressed in her own terms apart from the avenues provided by academia.

Silko's disappointment with graduate and professional schools did not prevent her from working within the academy. After dropping out of graduate school, she took a teaching job at Navajo Community College in Tsaile, Arizona, near the New Mexico state line and Canyon de Chelly. She recalls these days and her students fondly. Her writing continued to draw attention during this time, and she was awarded a Discover Grant from the National Endowment for the Arts. Her second son, Cazimir, was born in 1972. In 1974 Kenneth Rosen published seven of Silko's short stories in the aforementioned *Man to Send Rain Clouds: Contemporary Stories by American Indians*. That same year she published her only book of poetry, titled *Laguna Woman*. She also won a poetry award from *The Chicago Review* and later the Pushcart Prize for Poetry. In 1975 her short story "Lullaby" was selected as one of the 20 best short stories of the year and included in Martha Foley's *Best Short Stories of 1975*.

One might expect that a writer on the rise, as Silko was in the early seventies, would be keen to stay near the center of things so that she could continue making herself known. Instead, in 1973 Silko moved with her second husband, John Silko, to Ketchikan, Alaska, where she lived in an artist's residence on Ketchikan Creek while John worked for Alaskan Legal Services. This proved to be an influential period for her in several ways. For the first time in her life, she was away from her beloved Southwest. In fact, she probably could not have gone farther away in terms of differences in landscapes. One can see Silko exploring these contrasts in the short story "Storyteller," which is in the volume of the same name. In this story, set on the Kushkokwim River in Bethel, Alaska, a young woman enacts revenge upon a Gussuck, or white man, who had murdered her parents in an especially horrific way. Silko calls this her favorite story because of the characters she creates and the way that they reflect both interior and exterior landscapes. At the beginning of the story, we marvel with Silko as we try to imagine a landscape without lines. The colors of the sky and earth merge until no difference can ultimately be discerned between them: "It wasn't a good sign for the sky to be indistinguishable from the river ice, frozen solid and white against the earth. The tundra rose up behind the river but all the boundaries between the river and hills and sky were lost in the density of the pale ice."[7]

It is the interior landscapes of the characters, however, that drive the story. The young woman listens to her departed mother, who says she must tell the story of the murder: "It will take a long time, but the story must be told. There must not be any lies." The old man who lives with her conjures up his own story and "talked all winter, softly and incessantly about the giant polar bear stalking a lone man across the Bering Sea ice." Silko notes that merging the characters with a landscape unfamiliar to her was a challenge she met and one that moved her into another level of writing: "That's a big step for me, to go to a completely alien landscape. I managed. What I did in that story finally was to get the interior landscapes of the characters, and yet they are still related to the tundra and the river because that's how she does the guy in. I love that story because I like the characters and how she does the guy in."[8]

Clearly compelling to Silko, this story involves negotiating boundaries and identities represented by interior and exterior landscapes; these concerns were thrown into high relief when she moved to an unfamiliar place and endured several personal crises. In the biographical note to *Laguna Woman,* she writes: "1973 was a difficult year. There was a great deal of emotional turmoil in my life; I was trying to adjust to the rainy Alaskan coast" (*LW,* 44). A line from "Storyteller" about the story having to be told without any lies could be an epigraph to Silko's time in Alaska. Her most famous work, *Ceremony,* was a product of her struggles with the changes in climate, both physical and emotional. Silko's own story is perhaps reflected in the fact that she could write a novel that includes intricate descriptions of particular landscapes while she was more than a thousand miles away from those places. In fact, the writing of *Ceremony* turned out to be a kind of therapy for her depression: "Writing the novel was a ceremony for me to stay sane" (Fisher, 20). She recounts that she was having migraine headaches and nausea that would not go away. Tayo, the main character in the novel, is very sick at the beginning, and the larger story concerns if and how Tayo will be healed. As she thought about those in her family who, like Tayo, had returned from the war and had "made it" while others had not, she realized that writing was her own healing ceremony. As Tayo got better, she herself got better. Silko's integrity as a writer is manifested in the fact that she lived the very ceremony she was describing in the novel. She was cured by storytelling.

In 1978 Silko returned to Laguna and to the place where she had first been cradled by stories and land. *Ceremony* appeared in 1977, and she had wanted to get it into print as close as possible to the U.S. bicentennial celebration. In an interview conducted in 1976, she remarked: "I just want to make sure that during this year when all of this sort of celebrating is going on, that Americans can be reminded that there are different ways to look at the past 200 years. . . . In this Bicentennial year we should remember . . . that it was on this stolen land that this country was settled and begun."[9] This remark adeptly summarizes Silko's own sense of political activism; namely, she does her part by telling stories. In that same interview, she was asked about her opinion of the American Indian Movement (AIM).[10] Offering both criticisms and appreciations of AIM, she comments: "I feel it is more effective to write a story like 'Lullaby' than to rant and rave" (Seyersted, 24). Not coincidentally, Silko's observation that storytelling offers more potential for achieving justice recalls her earlier rationale for leaving law school.

Silko mentions her short story "Lullaby" as an example of how she perceives her political role. "Lullaby" is widely anthologized and has been read by many American students. It appears in *Storyteller,* Silko's third book. As the importance of *Ceremony* began to become clear to readers and critics, Silko continued her own brand of activism by combining Laguna myths and tales, local gossip, letters, commentary, and photographs into *Storyteller.* An autobiography in itself, it is a very personal statement presented in terms of stories and their tellers. There is also a political edge to the stories that cuts against the grain of American mythology, just as personal narratives by marginalized peoples who resist assimilation are inherently subversive. *Storyteller* stands in the tradition of autobiography as personal and political witness.

Silko continued to work with words and images by producing a film with the help of Dennis Carr called *Estoyehmuut and the Gunnadeyah,* or Arrowboy and the Destroyers, a story that appeared as one of the interwoven Laguna myths in *Ceremony.* In 1982 she produced a videotape titled *Running on the Edge of the Rainbow: Laguna Stories and Poems.* In addition to these projects, she began to take up photography as a way of exploring her new surroundings in Tucson.

Silko had moved to Tucson before the publication of *Storyteller*. Like her relocation to Alaska, this move was to have important consequences for her writing. Several personal and political events converged in Tucson in the 1980s that would emerge in her second novel, *Almanac of the Dead*. Silko became interested in the notion of time as it was conceived in ancient tribal cultures, especially the Mayan and Aztec. This interest led her to the ancient almanacs and codices of the Mayans, whose intricate ideas of time offered a sense of prophecy that was uncannily correct. For example, these books predicted the arrival of the explorer Cortez to the exact day. In the midst of these investigations, Silko was visiting with a friend who received a phone call from a woman who was looking for a psychic she had seen on television and who supposedly lived in Tucson. Right then, she relates, she started to think of a story where a young woman who had lost her child sought the aid of a psychic she had seen on television.

Combined with these interests was a fascination with snakes. With the move to Tucson, Silko had come upon many rattlesnakes in her exploration of the hills around her home. She says that they were friendly and curious about her. Interacting with these snakes started her thinking about Laguna stories of snakes, specifically Ma ah shra true ee, the sacred messenger, who will appear when the time of the whites is nearly over. In the spring of 1980, two employees of the Jackpile uranium mine near Paguate, just north of Laguna, were making their regular check of the premises when they discovered a "biomorphic configuration" near the huge piles of uranium tailings.[11] The configuration—over 30 feet long and 12 inches high—was that of a great stone snake whose head was pointed west with its jaws open wide. When Silko visited the site in 1980, she saw offerings of corn meal, pollen, coral, and turquoise sprinkled upon the snake's head. The appearance of the great stone snake generated various interpretations. Since the snake pointed its open mouth toward the next mesa it would devour, the more skeptical saw it as a sign that the mine and everything it represented had won the battle for the land. After the mine closed, however, the rumors were just the opposite: Ma ah shra true ee's message was that the time of the destroyers was passing. The great stone snake is a central feature of *Almanac of the Dead*.

After receiving a MacArthur Foundation grant, Silko began to write *Almanac of the Dead,* a labyrinthine and copious work of over 700 pages. In the 1980s, events in her personal life and in the communities of Laguna and Tucson coalesced to form the novel. She imagined a series of stories that would be modeled upon Mayan codices and include a great stone snake and a woman who seeks a psychic to help her find her lost child. It is not surprising that she wrote the novel in sections, not only because of the disparate elements of the plot but also because the remnants of the Mayan codices are themselves in sections. The motif that was to tie all these elements together was time. Silko explains: "I wanted to use narrative to shift the reader's experience of time and the meaning of history as stories that mark certain points in time. . . . I had to figure out how to do this and still tell stories people could understand. Myths alter our experience of time and reality without disappointing our desire for a story. I knew *Almanac of the Dead* must be made of myths—all sorts of myths from the Americas, including the modern myths" (*YWBS,* 140).

After writing these separate accounts of snakes, helicopter invasions of Tucson, and psychic quests, Silko was ready to try to put it all together. To accomplish this task, she decided that she needed to find a workplace separate from her home. Once again she moved. Although it was only to downtown Tucson, the transition, like the others, proved to have profound implications for her writing. She rented space from a lawyer in an old building on Stone Avenue where automatic rifle fire punctuated the night and homeless people congregated. It was, in Silko's words, "the United States of America that no one wants to talk about" (*YWBS,* 141). By 1985 she had over one thousand pages of *Almanac of the Dead,* and it still was not finished. By 1986 she was still writing feverishly and trying to get control of the characters to bring them to some end. With her five-year MacArthur Fellowship almost over, Silko asked her agent to sell the novel based on 660 pages of manuscript. Readers, critics, and friends had been eagerly awaiting the next Silko novel. In fact, she notes that she lost some friends during this period because she was almost completely immersed in the story.

It would be 1989 before she wrote the last sentence of *Almanac of the Dead.* The decade of the eighties had been spent with the characters and events of the novel in a kind of sacred time and space. Silko inhabited the stories in *Almanac* in ways that few writers do. She writes:

> I was a prisoner of my characters, who each day left me drained of all emotion and thought until I could barely interact with a clerk at the supermarket checkout counter. . . . Friends and family became concerned and then disappointed and angry. I couldn't blame them; by that time I really had spent so much time with my characters that they had in a way

replaced real human beings. Everyday human beings weren't nearly as exciting and interesting as my characters, either. Now that the novel is finished, I will have to begin trying to reintegrate myself into the real world; I will have to see if I have any friends remaining. (*YWBS*, 144–45)

Silko's odyssey in writing *Almanac of the Dead* is significant for her own story. The remarks she makes in interviews about storytelling being a way of life and constituting identity are not merely affectation. She lives the stories she tells as well as those that are told to her.

It is fitting, I think, to conclude this biographical sketch by relating one other episode from Silko's time on Stone Avenue. Frustrated by Arizona politics at the time and Governor Mecham in particular, Silko employed her passion for word, image, and story at Stone Avenue itself.[12] She began to work with a can of spray paint instead of a typewriter and moved outside to write. Her writing evolved into painting graffiti on one of the buildings on the street. Mastering the staccato form of this new medium, Silko wrote: "Recall Mecham. Impeach him. Indict him. Eat more politicians, end war, end taxes." The lawyer from whom she was renting her space let the graffiti stay until Mecham was recalled. Afterward the wall was whitewashed.

The story, however, does not end there. Silko decided to paint something nice for the people of the neighborhood on her newly created "canvas." She allowed her desire to paint to subsume her desire to finish the novel, and she let the manuscript sit for a few weeks as she turned to creating a Stone Avenue mural. The first image that came to her was that of a giant snake, which was suitable for the 40-foot wall that she was covering. The longer she worked on the mural, the better she felt about her writing, and so once again Silko was telling a story with words and images, a desire and talent that first surfaced with the publication of *Nasty Asty*. She observes: "As the mural began to work out beautifully, I realized it was somehow a sign to me that the novel would work out also, and I would be able to complete it successfully" (*YWBS*, 140). After completing the painting, she knew that she had the ending to her novel. The snake in the mural is a messenger who emerges from a rainstorm and is surrounded by flowers. In his stomach are skulls, and above his head are words in Spanish that appear to have blossomed from the flowers. In English the words read: "The people are hungry. The people are cold. The rich have stolen the land. The rich have stolen freedom. The people demand justice. Otherwise, Revolution." Whether producing a mural, photograph, poem, or novel, Leslie Marmon Silko weaves words and images together in ways that transgress the boundaries and identities drawn by destructive forces and integrate the power of the land and stories in creative ways.

Today Leslie Marmon Silko lives on her ranch outside Tucson and is working on a new novel titled *Garden in the Dunes,* which is about the experiences of two nineteenth-century Native American girls who are orphaned after the devastation of their tribe. She recently collected several essays and notes into the volume titled *Yellow Woman and a Beauty of the Spirit*. Her son Robert is a collector of rare books, and her younger son Cazimir plays music and writes science fiction. She continues to enjoy the solitude that she discovered on Stone Avenue. "A perfect day," she writes, "is a day spent watching my koi in their rainwater pool, playing with the macaws, and writing, drawing, and reading" (*LW,* 42).

Chapter Two

Laguna Woman:
The Poetry of Stories

Interpreting Native American Literature

Native American literature is different from other forms of literature. Although this observation may seem obvious, the fact of that difference needs to be noted. There are many cultural codes that announce this contrast, from special journals, conferences, courses, and programs in academia to special bookstore sections that contain anthologies, histories, and autobiographies that are considered Native American. In fact, the marketing of many of these ways of engaging Native American literature depends largely upon the fundamental assumption of its dissimilarity to other literatures, even mainstream "American" literature. Problems begin to occur, however, when a reader unfamiliar with Native American cultures begins to read Native American literature and is puzzled by this incongruity, which can be frustrating and alienating. In actuality, the difference that enticed one into reading in the first place can be exotic and interesting.

What is one to do when a Native American work presents a world radically different from the one that is expected by the nonnative reader? How do we respond to the creation of a world that is so close geographically but so far away culturally? More often than not, readers do what they always do, what is safe to do: They adjust the text to fit their strategies of reading rather than adjusting their reading strategies. Nonnative readers especially need to be aware of this problem and to allow their reading strategies to be criticized in the process of reading Native American texts. Crossing cultural boundaries, even literary ones, is a difficult and sometimes painful process, and without a willingness to adjust our expectations, reading across cultures can trivialize or exaggerate the distinctiveness of the other culture and simply reinforce our own beliefs about the world. It is crucial that we allow Native American literature to teach us and that we read in order to learn how to read. Otherwise, we will end up simply projecting our own cultural assumptions onto a body of work by people who do not share these assumptions, and in the end we will not have learned anything but how to drive our assumptions deeper into the background while a whole other world passes before our eyes.

Poetry is perhaps a better vehicle than fiction for announcing this difference. Readers familiar with Western poetry will either not find tropes and figures with which they are familiar—or they will find all them too easily. Early literary criticism of Native American poetry fell into this trap. One of the first volumes of Native American poetry is *Path on the Rainbow* (1918), edited by George W. Cronyn.[1] Mary Hunter Austin, a central figure in the interpretation of Native American poetry in the twentieth century, wrote in the introduction to Cronyn's anthology that there was an "extraordinary likeness" between Native poetry and that of the Imagists.[2] It was no accident, of course, that Imagism was alive and well in America when Austin made this observation. Paula Gunn Allen recounts a reading of one of Silko's poems in *Ceremony* that evidences the same assumptions. A critic analyzing the opening lines of the novel where Thought-Woman is sitting in her room, thinking of a story, proceeded to the interpretation that Silko considers herself to be Thought-Woman. Even a cursory knowledge of Laguna Pueblo mythology and culture would reveal that no storyteller would make that assumption. The critic's construction derives from ideas about propriety and creation that he or she brought to the text. As Allen points out, "the critic has removed the book and its author from the living web of the people and tradition from which they both arose."[3]

Interpreting Native American poetry in ways that do justice to the writers and texts is possible when the reader reads in order to learn and does so by learning to read. As Brian Swann notes in the introduction to a well-known anthology of Native American poetry, "Its full and generous presence in this volume will *announce* what it is in its own terms, using its own names."[4] What is called for is good listening, an attribute essential to storytelling. Listening means allowing a dialogue to emerge in which our assumptions and beliefs interact with the challenges to those beliefs offered by the story. It also means that we respect the storyteller and the factors and beliefs that produce her story.

Reading *Laguna Woman*

Silko is not widely known as a poet. Her reputation has been built upon short stories, such as "The Man to Send Rain Clouds," "Yellow Woman," and "Lullaby," and her two novels, *Ceremony* and *Almanac of the Dead*. Her poems have received some attention in discussions of *Storyteller,* and many critics have taken into account the poetic formulations of the Laguna stories in *Ceremony*. Almost none, however, have looked at Silko's poetry on its own as it appears in *Laguna Woman*. What we find in *Laguna Woman,* Silko's first published book, is the storytelling process at work in highly condensed form.[5]

Laguna Woman is a collection of 18 poems written in the early seventies while Silko was teaching at Navajo Community College in Tsaile, Arizona. Nine of these poems reappear in *Storyteller*. Published originally by Greenfield Review Press, *Laguna Woman* was republished in 1994 by Silko's own Flood Plain Press. Like the later *Storyteller* and *Sacred Water,* this book contains not only text but also drawings that represent animals, landscapes, and clouds. These black-and-white images (except for the cover drawing) use symbols common to southwestern iconography. Many of them take up the entire page, whereas others are found at the ends of the poems, and two pages have spiders crawling across them.

These poems are stories and contain many of the intriguing elements that we find in Silko's other writings. Laguna gossip, myth, and landscape figure prominently as does the landscape around Chinle and Tsaile, Arizona. Dominated by animals, colors, and weather, the poems nonetheless center on human concerns like love and sex. Several of these works are winter poems and are concerned with crackling ice, blinding white skies, and the scarcity of food. Combined with Silko's innate storytelling abilities is a capacity to evoke particular settings and emotions by the juxtaposition of concepts and images, such as butterflies dying softly or a snow wolf exploding gray ice dreams of eternity. A concern with the self in Silko's verse suggests deep introspection.

The form of these poems is worth noting. First of all, 11 of them have epigraphs that indicate time and often place. For example, in "Four Mountain Wolves" the epigraph reads: "Chinle late winter, 1973 when the wolves came." When specified, the place is always somewhere in the Navajo nation. The epigraphs, though they might be considered extraneous to some, subtly locate the reader in time and space and tie the poems to particular landscapes at particular times. Silko's use of epigraphs reflects an important aspect of Native American concepts of time and space. Many Native cultures understand time not as an abstract notion but as intimately tied to experience, particularly the knowledge of a place.[6] Silko likes to use stanzas, and seven of these poems' stanzas vary in length from 2 to 10 lines, conveying to the

reader the sense that some sort of orchestrated movement is at work. In fact, such motion is at the heart of Silko's storytelling technique. Whether she is writing *Almanac of the Dead* like a Mayan codex or creating a gradually emerging pattern in *Ceremony,* Silko is always weaving, tying together disparate strands of experience into a web of meaning. The stanza format highlights this technique. Finally, with regard to form, readers should take note of the cascading lines and the spacing between both words and lines. White space for Silko generally means strategic pauses that would ordinarily be found in an oral setting. Silko has stated that she tries—with her unique use of spacing—to recreate on the page the dynamics of oral speech as she heard it in the stories her relatives told: "I play around with the page by using different kinds of spacing or indentations or even italics so that the reader can sense, say, that the tone of the voice has changed. If you were hearing a story, the speed would increase at certain points. I want to see how much I can make the page communicate those nuances and shifts to the reader" (Barnes, 50). It is clear that Silko is attempting to evoke a sense of presence where readers enter the world of the stories and then undertake the journeys they find.

Reading *Laguna Woman* is a journey that begins with a drive from Chinle to Fort Defiance for an abortion. Next is a coyote story that involves several incarnations of coyote preying upon various groups of people, including whites. Then come poems about love, friendship, and family, including ancestors from 700 years ago. Animals appear prominently in the next few poems, and then we are treated to two poems that derive from tribal gossip about adultery. The next few verses invoke mythological themes from origins to journeys and visitations. The book concludes with poems about docile horses drinking from a water trough after a long day's work and a ritual gathering of crows who have assembled to pick clean the carcass of a sheep killed on the highway. There is, then, a sense of having traveled through land and life after reading *Laguna Woman*. The book is a sustained rumination upon relationships: of people to animals, of animals to each other, of people to land and sky, and of people to each other. We recognize a deep interest in boundaries: how they are drawn, how they blur, and how identity stems from these boundaries and changes over time and circumstance.

For the purposes of analysis, the poems can be divided into three types: those concerning journeys and time, those focusing on animals, and those concerned with love and sex. These distinctions are arbitrary, however, since in many of the poems, the themes merge in engaging ways.

Poems of Journeys and Time

The first poem in the book is titled "Poem for Myself and Mei-Mei: Concerning Abortion." The epigraph reads: "Chinle to Fort Defiance, April, 1973." Mei-Mei is Silko's longtime friend Mei-Mei Berssenbrugge, herself a poet. The poem is told in four stanzas and is accompanied by a drawing of what appears to be a sunflower, although it might also be an embryo. The stanzas correspond roughly to the drive to Fort Defiance and the return home. The first verse speaks of the morning sun, the second focuses on winter and spring, the third stands apart from the others and mentions a horse by the highway, and the fourth speaks of dying butterflies. Because the epigraph describes a drive of some 75 miles on the Navajo reservation, this is a journey poem, the last words of which describe the fluttering of wings "all the way home."

A recurring image in "Poem for Myself and Mei-Mei" is that of butterflies, and the words concern how they live and die. The butterflies are yellow, an important color in the Southwest that connects with the sun and corn among other things. In fact, it is Yellow Woman in Laguna mythology who embodies aspects of the sun and corn and who is one of the most important figures for Silko. As we shall see in Silko's short story of the same name, Yellow Woman is the journeying heroine, the one who leaves home and family to find love, sex, and adventure in other parts of the land. Yellow Woman appears in much of Silko's work, and she is in this poem as well. We read in the first stanza that "The morning sun / coming unstuffed with yellow light" is "butterflies tumbling loose / and blowing across the Earth." The narrator sees them "with the clarity of ice" that has been shattered in mountain streams, and in these streams the pebbles are "alive beneath the water." In this stanza life in all its forms is seen with perfect clarity, but by the end of the poem that distinctness will dim.

The second stanza shifts the scene and tense to a past winter when "it snowed / mustard grass / and springtime rained it." Here the butterflies are "yellow mustard flowers / spilling out of the mountain." Although the tense stays the same, the colors and images change in the short third stanza. A white horse stands out because he is scratching his rump on a tree. This, too, is life, although it is not as majestic as butterflies or flowers. Returning to the present tense in the fourth stanza, we also return to the image of the butterflies who are now dying softly on the windshield of the car, and "the iridescent wings / flutter and cling / all the way home."

The prominent elements here are the sky, the butterflies, and the lens through which the narrator sees them. At the beginning there is the clarity of shattered ice in mountain streams through which she can see the magnificence of the butterflies tumbling loose from the sun and filling the sky. Life continues in the winter and spring in the form of mustard grass, whose seeds fall from the sky. In the third stanza the vision is not of sky or earth but of a white horse scratching his rear end on a tree. This rather uninspiring action stands in sharp contrast to the more mythical images of butterflies spilling from the earth and sky. The sharp contrast continues into the last stanza where the butterflies are now dying, caught by the car's windshield that holds their colorful wings all the way home. The lens of ice has been replaced by a dirty windshield, and the butterflies are dead.

It is too easy to equate the butterflies with the fetus. This is not an antiabortion poem; rather, the sense that we are left with at the end is that the butterflies will return because they are made of sun and grass. The sunflower drawing at the bottom of the page reinforces this idea. The first two stanzas ruminate upon life and beauty, the last two upon ugliness and death, but in the end the reader knows that these are entwined just as the parts of the poem are. The reader also realizes that she has been on a journey not only from Chinle to Fort Defiance but also through the cycle of life and death. "Poem for Myself and Mei-Mei" examines the beauty and loss occasioned by the passing of time.

Another example of Silko's ability to weave disparate images is found in "Toe'osh: A Laguna Coyote Story," which is dedicated to Simon J. Ortiz, a prominent writer from Acoma Pueblo near Laguna. This poem comprises eight stanzas, and the subject is Coyote in his many manifestations. Renowned for his exploits in trickery, concupiscence, and curiosity, Coyote is, of course, a legendary figure in Pueblo and other Native American mythologies. In short, Coyote is too smart for his own good. Coyote stories, as well as other Pueblo tales, are often told in the company of many listeners. The fire or stove is a natural gathering place for storytelling, and it is this setting that provides the backdrop for "Toe'osh: A Laguna Coyote Story." The poem begins on a winter night when people have gathered to hear coyote stories, and their stories this night center on elements in Coyote's life, such as how sparrows stuck bits of old fur on him with pitch to create his "ratty old fur coat" after he lost his "proud original one" in a bet. The second stanza recounts a Navajo story in which Coyote actually wins something. In a contest with chipmunk, badger, and skunk to see who could stay outside the longest, Coyote tricks them by going inside after they are asleep and then going back outside before they wake up. Stanza three is Silko's own Coyote story that probably refers to her great-grandfather Robert and his brother Walter. These men and those who accompanied them were white Presbyterian missionaries who came to Laguna in the late 1800s to evangelize and work as surveyors. They married Laguna women, such as Grandmother Anaya, and settled permanently in the area. Silko's third stanza speaks of white men coming to Laguna and nearby Acoma "a hundred years ago" and fighting over land and women. She writes: "Even now / some of their descendants are howling in / the hills southeast of Laguna."

Because he cannot resist trying to fulfill all his cravings at once, Coyote is funny and instructive. He wants sex, food, and sleep in abundance but has no sense of how to balance these desires. In the next few stanzas of the Toe'osh poem, Silko explores these desires in contemporary Laguna politics. Charlie Coyote runs for governor and proclaims that when elected he plans to run all the men off the reservation in order to keep the women to himself. Other coyotes in the form of Laguna politicians campaign elaborately, going door to door handing out turkeys and hams in exchange for promises of votes. Like Coyote, however, they are tricked because "[o]n election day all the people / stayed home and ate turkey / and laughed." The vice-president of the Trans-Western pipeline who came to Laguna to negotiate for a right-of-way falls prey to the trickery of Coyote when the Lagunas leave the vice-president waiting until the afternoon and then tell him to come back tomorrow. In the seventh stanza, the penultimate, Silko retells the story of coyotes who were standing on a high mesa watching a festival of dancers who had food spread out in abundance. The leader of this band of coyotes is the title character, Toe'osh. The immediate problem for him and his cousins is how to get down the mesa. They decide to make a coyote chain by holding one another's tails in their mouths until the chain reaches the bottom of the mesa. This idea works fine until one in the middle breaks wind. The unfortunate coyote holding the offensive tail opens his mouth to complain about the bad odor, and they all fall down.

The final stanza returns honor to Toe'osh by telling how he "scattered white people / out of bars all over Wisconsin." Howling and roaring, he keeps bumping into white people coming out of bars until they say "Excuse me." The last line is telling and puts a fine point on the poem: "And the way Simon meant it / was for 300 or maybe 400 years." Toe'osh is loved because he instructs and entertains. With the last line of the poem, however, we learn that he has a political function as well: It takes a trickster to get white people to apologize. This trickster is some-one whose nonconformist actions are frightening enough to eke some grudging remorse out of the ones who stole the land. The line "Excuse me" serves both to reverse the flow of power and to create a language outside the dominant culture. The imaginary white person in the poem does not mean his excuse to be for all the atrocities committed against Native Americans, but Toe'osh's character, as it develops in the stories, allows us to imagine a larger tale in which that is in fact the case. The line also refers to Simon Ortiz as a trickster with poetic power.

The majestic "Prayer to the Pacific" describes a journey the narrator takes to the ocean "distant / from my southwest land of sandrock." The sight of the immense ocean is overwhelming, and the only appropriate simile is that the moving blue water is as "big as the myth of origin." The narrator imagines the pale water reaching all the way to the sun that floats west to China "where the ocean herself was born." Clouds are important to life in the Southwest because they bring rain, and in this poem the clouds that blow across the sand are wet. The narrator, whom we easily imagine as Silko, squats in the wet sand, talks to the ocean, and offers it the turquoise and red coral that it sent east. Consistent with the Laguna tendency (at least before Spanish contact) to see goddesses rather than gods, the narrator sees the ocean as a sister spirit of the earth much as the sky is a sister spirit of the earth. She then picks up four round stones to "carry back the ocean / to suck and to taste." The narra-tor recalls a story that tells of Indians riding giant sea turtles across the ocean 30,000 years ago. "As the old people say," the ocean still gives its gifts in the form of rain clouds that drift east from the ocean. In the midst of green leaves and with wet earth on her feet, the narrator speaks of "swallowing raindrops / clear from China." "Prayer to the Pacific" typifies the Laguna interest in stories that have global, not just paro-chial, import.

Immediately following this poem is one of the most complex in the collection by virtue of its multidimensionality. "Indian Song: Survival" exemplifies a prominent theme in the poems in *Laguna Woman,* namely, the erotic nature of hunting and the blending of the desires for food and sex. This poem is told in 10 stanzas that provide a series of snapshots of the predator and prey. The narrator here is one of a group of Indians who have ironically gone north to escape winter. They climb pale cliffs and sleep beside the river. The image that comes to mind is of the ancient ancestors of the Pueblo people, the Anasazi, climbing out of their cliffside homes and heading north to escape the scarcities of winter. They are followed by "mountainlion man," who sleeps in the branches of the river willows and waits for his chance to pounce. Mountainlion man speaks to the narrator in the eighth stanza to tell her that she "can't sleep with the river forever. / Smell winter and know." In the final stanza the hunt has merged into a sexual union. "You lay beside me in the sunlight," it reads, "and / you ask me if I still smell winter." The answer comes amid the forest wind in the form of an invitation for mountainlion man to taste her because she is the wind and to touch her because she is "the lean grey deer / running on the edge of the rainbow." "Indian Song" uses images drawn from the Yellow Woman story as well. Yellow Woman meets a hunter by the river who takes her away, and in the poem," the narrator sinks her body into the shallow sand of the cold river, a river that is "warmer than any man."

"Slim Man Canyon" was written for Silko's first husband, John, and echoes the theme of a journey across time. In this case the time is "700 years ago," a line that begins the poem and is set off at the left margin and repeated as the last line set off at the right margin. The phrase is repeated twice in the middle of the poem. The time period indicates that here, too, Silko is imagining her Anasazi ancestors who lived where "water was running gently / and the sun was warm / on pumpkin flowers." She immediately connects this place with her own beginnings by noting that "[w]here I come from is like this." The journey takes the narrator and her companion "past cliffs with stories and songs / painted on rock / 700 years ago." This is a rumination upon time and space and how, despite the accumulation of calendar time, the sense of place has not changed. The water, the sun, the sandstone, the silence, the willow smell, and the rhythm of the horses' feet all continue as they have for all time. Calendar time cannot screen out the reality of simultaneity, the coming together of different times in one place.

Poems Concerning Animals

Animals play an important role in Native American mythology and literature. In particular, Laguna mythology contains the *hummah-hah* stories of a time when animals and human beings shared a common language. Silko refers to these stories frequently as a basis for her work. Not surprisingly, many animals appear in *Laguna Woman*. They relate with humans in ways that dissolve the differences between humans and animals, and this relationship is central to Silko's work. When asked what she wanted to make accessible to her readers, Silko replied: "Things about relationships. That's all there really is. . . . I'll come back after a wonderful day [walking in the hills], and someone will say that place is full of snakes. And I just had the feeling that there wouldn't be any problem with snakes and there wasn't. . . . Relationships are not just limited to man-woman, parent-child, insider-outsider; they spread beyond that" (Fisher, 22). Animals appear frequently in Silko's poetry, fiction, and art in order for her to explore this particular connection.

A poem that speaks of animals and humans in relation to each other describes the appearance of "Four Mountain Wolves." In late winter of 1973 these wolves apparently came into Silko's view. Devoting a stanza to each wolf, she gives names to the first three that reflect their color and some aspect of the landscape they represent. The last wolf in the fourth stanza is described in a different fashion: This wolf is lean and running, unlike the others, who are gray or white and look like mist or snow. Each wolf's name begins each stanza at the extreme left of the page with the lines immediately following cascading down and to the right.

"Grey mist wolf" is introduced in the first stanza. This wolf moves southwest from a frozen mountain lake and sings "Ah ouoo." He wades through fog that is belly high and laments the fact that the deer are all gone. No doubt the fog would provide excellent cover for hunting if there were anything to hunt. He is lonely for deer and turkey who have gone away. In his loneliness he follows the edge of the sun and waits for the faint light to reveal prey. The next wolf is "Swirling snow wolf," who spills "the yellow-eyed wind / on blue lake stars / Orion / Saturn." This wolf sounds powerful:

> tear the heart from the silence
> rip the tongue from the darkness
> Shake the earth with your breathing
> explode grey ice dreams of eternity. (17)

His voice booms violently as it cuts through the silence and darkness and shatters any sense we might have of a timeless winter. He is alive and lets everyone know.

Stanza III introduces either a wolf with two names or perhaps two different wolves: "Mountain white mist wolf" and "Grey fog wolf." The first has frozen crystals on his silver hair, and his breath is a "steaming silver mist from his mouth." "Grey fog wolf" travels through the years to Black Mountain. This wolf is said to "call to the centuries" on a "howling wolf wind," and those animals and humans who hear this call fear it and "huddle in the distances / weak." If these are indeed two different wolves, then there are five (not four) mountain wolves. It may be that Silko means to give two different names to the wolf in the third stanza, or she may not include in her count the very different wolf in the last stanza. "Lean wolf running" in the final stanza shares none of the other wolves' majesty. This wolf is hungry and scurrying to find prey; perhaps he is near starvation. For this wolf the "miles become faded in time," and desire is his constant companion. He dreams the dream of "Green eyes wolf" (another wolf not accounted for) when she approaches an elk softly, "her pale lavender outline / startled into eternity." This wolf also demonstrates one of the themes of *Laguna Woman:* the equation of birth and death with food and sex. The elk's belly is swollen as if she is about to give birth, but we know that she is in fact about to be killed, "startled into eternity." The hunt is undertaken and consummated by the desire to satisfy the appetites of hunger and sex.

In order to personalize these mountain wolves, Silko places each one into his own story containing cosmological elements. Grey mist wolf follows the edge of the sun, Swirling snow wolf shakes the earth with his breathing and spills the wind on the stars Orion and Saturn, the wolf or wolves in the third stanza call to the centuries, and Lean wolf running watches the miles fade in time. The description of each wolf actualizes him for the reader. We can almost see the breath of Mountain white mist wolf as a steaming silver mist or hear Swirling snow wolf tear the heart from the silence. At the same time, these are mythical wolves who populate the cosmos like gods. The effect of their actions is felt in the vast reaches of time and earth.

There is a strong sense of many things converging in this poem, from the stars in the blue lake above to the deer who have gone down to the valley, from the majestic presence of the mountain wolves to the stark hunger that rouses them to sing, howl, and run in order to bewail their plight or to find food. The overwhelming theme at work is time, as we saw in the previous poems. Swirling snow wolf explodes "grey ice dreams of eternity." Grey mist wolf follows "the edge of the sun." Grey fog wolf has "travelled the years," and Lean wolf running dreams of an elk "startled into eternity." The timeless character of the wolves is balanced by the demands of time, namely, food. These wolves are not visions; rather, they are figures bound by time. They explode our attempt to make them timeless and speak to us instead of real fear as we huddle weakly in the distances. Silko describes a powerful visitation by the wolves but refuses to reify them into abstract archetypes. They are as real as time and cold and hunger. They are not eternal by virtue of being timeless; instead, they are eternal by being full of time.

One of the volume's more tightly woven poems—titled "Preparations"—also implies a certain awareness of time and describes a gathering of crows who devour a dead sheep, presumably killed by a car, beside the highway. The highway provides the speaker with a front-row seat to the ceremony being conducted by the crows. The sheep's belly is "burst open," implying a violent death such as that produced by impact with a car. We see, as if we were in the car, the sheep's "guts and life unwinding on the sand." In fact the narrator invites us to "look at the long black wings / the shining eyes" of the solemn and fat crows who have come together to carefully attend the body and "to make preparations." They gradually work downward, pulling wool from skin, picking meat from bone, and then tendon from muscle. Laboring patiently, they remark to each other that in a few more days the carcass will be finished. It finally is finished, and the crows part with the benediction "Bones, bones / Let wind polish the bones. / It is done."

The poem represents a snapshot of life on the planet feeding on other life. This is not, however, a poem about the brutality of nature or a survival-of-the-fittest parable. Instead, it ritualizes an act that passing motorists would no doubt deem excessive and repulsive. "The body is carefully attended," not treated as roadkill. It serves a purpose, and the crows and the narrator recognize this fact. The belly, like the belly of the elk in the previous poem and like that in *Ceremony,* is the seat of life and of the story. The belly contains "guts and life," and for it to spill its contents upon the road is for it to tell a story. As the crows consume this story, it becomes their life, their story. Preparations are involved because something sacred is going on. Even the wind has its role to play as it comes in at the end to polish the bones and announce the end of the story and the ceremony.

Another ceremony is described in "Where Mountainlion Lay Down with Deer." Silko describes her entrance into a world apart from her everyday existence: the world of Black Rock Mountain. In this world time flows differently, and the speaker finds herself "stepping from day to day / silently." As she returns up a cliff that she descended a thousand years ago, she smells the wind for a "crushed mountain smell" of "pale blue leaves," the scent of her ancestors. There she finds a faded black stone that marks the place where mountainlion lay down with deer. She decides that it is better to stay there "watching wind's reflection / in tall yellow flowers" than to return to her accustomed world, at least for the time being. The old ones are all gone, those who remember her and the story of her birth. Gone also is her dancing in the moonlight and swimming away in freezing mountain water. The water is memory itself tumbling down out of the mountain stone "spilling out / into the world." The narrator sees herself as the offspring of the mountain-lion and the deer, and once again Silko evokes the image of predator and prey as a moment of sexual desire. In climbing the mountain and "stepping from day to day," she retraces the path of the water, her memory, as it flows out into the world.

"Hawk and Snake" offers a similar journey through time and memory as the speaker walks slowly away from houses and stores, looking back only once or twice at the distant fields and fences. As she looks ahead, her perspective changes, and she begins to see the immensity of the sky, which is "blue beyond all else / blue, light / above the pale red earth." Continuing in her trek away from the civilized world and toward this new perception, she begins to recall that there are others here, such as Snake and Hawk. The snake is coiled "on his rocks," and the hawk is "soaring / silent arcs above the canyon." Suddenly, this reality disappears, and there is "no longer / blue flower, spiral rock / spring water." Instead she is "back again," only this time she sweeps "high above the hills / on brown spotted wings" and peers out from rocks as she is "coiled in the noontime shade." This poem describes a journey "back again" to a place that belongs to the animals and from which the narrator derives a new perspective—that of Hawk and Snake—on the place she lives.

The idea that the animals own certain places appears in the poem "The Time We Climbed Snake Mountain." Once again the narrator climbs a mountain, this time with companions. She feels the mountain as she scrambles along and finds good places for her hands as she grabs "the warm parts of the cliff." Being pressed against the warm earth reminds her that yellow spotted snake is "sleeping on his rock in the sun" nearby. This short poem ends with the narrator turning to her companions to tell them to

> watch out,
>   don't step on the spotted yellow snake
>   he lives here
>   The mountain is his.

The idea that the land belongs to the animals appears in other poems. In two of these poems Silko imagines epiphanies where animals appear out of the landscape itself and bring with them gifts of the land. "In Cold Storm Light" describes a scene in which the narrator is watching a canyon rim and smelling a wind wet with piñon that carries the sound of juniper. To set off the dramatic appearance of something new, Silko includes the two-word line "AND THEN." The vision is of snow elk "running swiftly / pounding / swirling above the tree tops." They are a "white song" and a "storm wind." Once past, they leave behind a "crystal trail of snowflakes" and "strands of mist" that become tangled in rocks and leaves. In "Sun Children" the epiphany is wild ducks floating on the north wind. In the first stanza the ducks are flying south "ahead of winter" to the "Sun House." In the second stanza "The ducks come again singing," and they bring along the strong sun whose "beauty grows inside us / around us." The sun children bring spring and life to the frozen water and "fragments of winter light."

Silko's vision of animals brings them to the same level as human beings. They perform ceremonies, tell stories, and want food and sex. They cry when they do not have these desires fulfilled and are grateful when they are. The animal poems and themes in *Laguna Woman* take us back to a time or a place where the differences between animals and humans have been dampened in favor of larger similarities. This time and place echoes that of the *hummah-hah* stories, where animals and humans conversed in the same language. In *Laguna Woman,* that language is the language of story and ceremony, of hunger and sex, and of birth and death.

Poems Concerning Love and Sex

We have already seen the theme of love and sex explored in the poems about journeys and time, such as "Indian Song: Survival," and in the poems about animals, such as "Four Mountain Wolves." We have noted that the journey taken by animals and humans is consummated at times in both erotic and predatory terms. There are, however, several poems in the collection in which the theme of love and sex dominates in unique ways.

Written in June of 1973, "When Sun Came to Riverwoman" is a poem that evokes the mystical quality of a creation myth and combines it with the pain of lost love. It is one of the most poignantly beautiful of all of Silko's poems. The structure of the poem follows the familiar story of Yellow Woman down by the river who is visited and overwhelmed by a male figure, Buffalo Man, the Gambler, or in this case, the sun himself. Images of spring run through the poem like the muddy, fast water. This spring is also timeless, "the year unknown / unnamed," and at the end the reader feels that time and timelessness have been stitched together in a moment captured by the sun at the Rio Grande.

The poem begins in lowercase letters with "that time / in the sun / beside the Rio Grande," and the typical cascading pattern is used with the first line on the left and the next two lines indented to the right. In three lines the reader is presented with a distinct image that evokes a particular time and place and from which a mythical account of intercourse will emerge. The next lines add sound to the scene with the voice of the mourning dove calling "long ago long ago / remembering the lost one / remembering the love." These lines prompt us to believe that the events that are about to be described have already happened and that this poem will be about a past encounter that the speaker is recalling with some melancholy. The next few lines move the scene into a timeless state where "Out of the dense green / eternity of springtime / willows rustle in the blue wind" and the year is "unknown / unnamed." Again, timelessness here does not mean untouched by time but rather so full of time that time appears to be endless. The water described is a perfect metaphor for this notion: The river is both constant and constantly changing. It is also muddy and fast and warm around the speaker's feet. The intercourse begins when the sun moves slowly into the current and caresses the speaker's "brown skin thighs" as she feels "deep intensity / flowing water." His warmth spreads to the yellow sand and sky. The erotic nature of their contact carries them into a different temporal dimension. Now there are "endless eyes shining always." At the same time the dove will not let her forget; it continues to cry out in a mourning wail as if to remind her that, like the water, this moment will pass. Nothing in this poem is timeless in the sense of being untouched by time, but the encounter of sun and riverwoman is a moment that seems to hold all time even though the moment itself passes. The speaker realizes that the dove's message about time passing "is ordained / in the swirling brown water," and it carries away the sun, her "lost one," her love.

The conclusion of the poem recapitulates the "time in the sun":

man of sun
    came to riverwoman
    and in the sundown wind
  he left her
     to sing
       for rainclouds swelling in the northwest sky
       for rainsmell on pale blue winds
                    from China.

Many of the themes of *Laguna Woman* converge in this marvelous conclusion. The poem is about the sun's journey to the west after his erotic and fruitful encounter with the earth and the river and about the lamentation occasioned by his passing. Her singing over the loss of the sun creates life-giving rain clouds in the northwest sky and the wonderful smell of rain on the pale blue winds. While the river carries the sun away over the mountain, the wind sends back his timeless gifts of water. The water departs in the river and returns in the clouds. The sacred encounter of sun and riverwoman is fleeting, but it will reoccur and produce life once more.

Two other poems are less mystical and more direct about love and sex. Written in 1972, "Si'ahh aash' " and "Mesita Men" reflect the kind of Laguna gossip that we read about in *Storyteller*. Silko writes about sexual mores in Laguna in an essay titled "Yellow Woman and A Beauty of the Spirit." She remarks, "Sexual inhibition did not begin until the Christian missionaries arrived. For the old-time people, marriage was about teamwork and social relationships, not about sexual excitement. In the days before the Puritans came, marriage did not mean an end to sex with people other than your spouse. Women were just as likely as men to have a *si'ash,* or lover" (*YWBS*, 67). In reading these two brief poems, we feel as if we are in the kitchen with two women sharing some juicy information about lovers. A footnote tells us that *Si'ahh aash'* is a Laguna word that means "the man you are sleeping with who is not your husband."

"Si'ahh aash' " is told in two stanzas. The first employs the perspective of two speakers who see another woman pass by: "There goes one / that's sleeping with him." They wonder how many that makes and guess that it is about 15 or 20. This conclusion prompts the line "He's got more women / than some men got horses." In the second stanza the voice turns to Si' ahh aash' and accuses him in a flattering way:

> How easy it is for you
>
> > > Si' ahh aash'
>
> > all us pretty women
>
> > > in love with you.

This brief, gossipy poem is packed with social information and ideas about love in Laguna. Noticeably absent is any sense of moralizing or judgment. In fact if there is anything at work here it is a kind of appreciation for the dynamics of sexuality and love and how they tend to overcome and transgress any boundaries. The sexual attractiveness and accomplishments of Si' ahh aash' are compared to the accumulation of wealth in terms of horses, and this man has more women than horses. "How easy it is for you" is not a statement of blame or jealousy. Instead, there is a sense of admiration for a man who has "all us pretty women" in love with him. The woman who is speaking knows that she has a similar power: She is pretty and shares in the delightful transgression for the sake of love, beauty, and pleasure. She feels some strange sense of community with the woman passing by, only one of 15 or 20 who are a part of this ritual. This is a community of Yellow Women who are enticed by the possibilities of love and adventure to go off with a beautiful man.

"Mesita Men" is shorter and more direct. "They feed you chili stew," and "Then they want / to fuck you." Here the connection between food and sex is explicit, direct, and succinct. The men of Mesita translate the hunt for food directly into a hunt for sex and see the exchange as an even one. The drawing that accompanies this five-line poem dominates the page, taking up nearly three-quarters of it. On the left is a creature of some kind with an almost metallic appearance and machinelike qualities. It appears to have antennae and a long tail and to be standing on two feet. Its head looks like a helmet, and a long protrusion resembles a nose with whiskers on it. The lines on this proboscis, however, are straight, and it is constructed of three rectangles. Even the whiskerlike features are straight lines. The most obvious property of this creature is a protrusion that extends from its midsection across the page, through an angular object and into the center of a round figure surrounded by eight small rectangles on its border. The phallic and yonic symbolism are obvious, but there is also more at work. The round figure may be a bowl of chili stew as well as a vagina. The angular figure itself passes through at least part of the phallic protrusion of the creature on the left and suggests intercourse. The drawing highlights the connections between food and sex that we have seen throughout the poetry in this volume.

Another poem in the collection concerning the theme of love and sex is appropriately titled "Love Poem" and was written in the late spring of 1972. It is framed by the line "rain smell comes with the wind," which appears both at the beginning and end of the poem. An element that appears frequently in the poems in *Laguna Woman*, rain smell expands the reader's sense of place by incorporating the olfactory sense, which is not usually exercised in poetry. This particular poem is about celebrating the senses, for along with the smell of rain we read of the smell of sand dunes, the sight of "tall grass glistening / in the rain," and "warm raindrops." The senses come alive with summer, and we "smell of her breathing new life." The senses are life itself and also erotic; hence the title of the poem refers not only to a man, who appears only near the end, but also to creation itself and the possibility of experiencing the "body" of the earth in this woman's body. In fact, the phrase "this woman" appears parenthetically in two places in the poem and in another place without parentheses. It is as if to say that this woman, one particular female, is a matrix through which the summer itself passes, and the sensations she feels in this experience are like the touch of a lover. The eroticism of the poem builds gradually. At first there are the smells, then "whispering to dark wide leaves / white moon blossoms dripping / tracks in the sand." Finally, the desire is stated clearly: "I am full of hunger / deep and longing to touch / wet tall grass, green and strong beneath." In the next lines the desire is consummated: "This woman loved a man / and she breathed to him / her damp earth song." Echoing the sentiment of the lost sun in "When Sun Came to Riverwoman," the narrator of "Love Poem" tells us that she is haunted by this story and remembers it in the cottonwood leaves and in the wide blue sky "when the rain smell comes with the wind."

In addition to poems of love and sex, there is also a poem of friendship, written in the early spring of 1973 and titled "Poem for Ben Barney." The poem celebrates the power and ability of words to call forth land and life. "If the time ever came / I would call you / and you would come," Silko writes, and then they would stand on separate mountain tops and call the meadows and mountains, the winds of the earth, one-legged antelope, and crow and his chorus. The convergence of voices summons forth a harmonious display of life on the land, including the "flute man coming from the distances." All these characters are "leaping and dancing lightly" in the "sunshine not yet ended / sunshine not yet through." The drawing opposite this poem includes inverted mountains with rain clouds and a female figure cradled in a flowering plant. This poem is not only about words in and of themselves but also about words in dialogue and harmony and about the power that is evoked when they merge, when they "summon together."

Laguna Woman and the poems in *Storyteller* place Silko in the company of great Native American poets like Joy Harjo, Linda Hogan, Carter Revard, Louise Erdrich, Gail Tremblay, Ray Young Bear, James Welch, Duane Niatum, Gerald Vizenor, and Jimmie Durham. Yet *Laguna Woman* has not received the critical attention that is due it, perhaps because of the attention given to Silko's novels and short fiction. Like her fiction, however, these poems offer a vision of the world that is radically different from that provided by dominant American mythologies. In the world of the poems, animals are not hierarchically different from humans, sex is very much like hunting and vice-versa, and human beings and animals do not attempt to escape time but relish its fullness. Here is a vision of the world that privileges place and the orbit of time, people, and stories around particular places. Above all, these poems are about relationships—how humans, animals, and stories live with and reflect the land and how the land contains them all. Silko perceives her writing as a gift to the earth. *Laguna Woman* is one of her finest offerings and reflects genuine humility as well as adoration for the mother who holds the stories.

Chapter Three
Ceremony: Healing with Stories

Leslie Marmon Silko's work is about the importance of stories, how they orient one in the world and how they keep people and cultures alive. Without stories the world becomes fragmented, and its people, alienated. *Ceremony* is a story about stories and their power to heal. The novel does not present stories as the unshakable final truth or a Platonic ideal. On the contrary, readers of the novel are privy to the delicacy of stories as well as their strength. Like spider webs, their fragility derives from their individual strands, and their strength results from their connection to other stories. *Ceremony* is itself such a web, bringing together many different narrative strands in a complex relationship of stories, characters, and land. In the end, however, we see the pattern that has been spun out of Spider Woman's belly, and all things are interconnected.

Ceremony is a multidimensional work in both form and content. The opening pages of the novel are not prose but verse and speak of Thought-Woman "sitting in her room and whatever she thinks about appears." Thought-Woman is also the spider, the grandmother of all life. From these opening pages we learn about the energy of stories, their ability to cure, and their capacity to counter the witchery of destruction. These verse forms appear throughout the novel and contain stories from Laguna mythology about how crises are handled and problems solved. There are obvious and not-so-obvious connections between the main character's experiences and the events in the verse stories. These connections will be explored in the next section.

Another important aspect of the form of the novel is the use of line breaks and spacing. As noted earlier, Silko is attempting to translate oral storytelling to the printed page, so we should take note of these unusual spacings. Clearly, line breaks indicate pauses in the story, and extra spacings indicate longer, perhaps dramatic, pauses. For example, the spacing in the opening "poem" of the novel represents a specific storytelling style according to the line breaks and extra spacing.

> Ts'its'tsi'nako, Thought-Woman,
> is sitting in her room

and whatever she thinks about

appears.[1]

If this poem is read aloud and the cues given by the breaks are incorpo-
rated into the speech, listeners can perceive a distinct style. There is a
rhythm to the words, a cadence that marks the story as a personal one
even as it performs its communal function. If the word *appears* were
included in the line above it, the meaning would change. As it is, the
word set off on its own line indicates that the appearing is as magical as
the thinking. A more telling use of spacing occurs at the end of this initial poem with the word *sunrise,* which shows up by itself at the bottom
of the final page of the poem just before the prose narration begins. The
effect involves a striking appearance of white that requires a slight
adjustment of the eye as it takes in the almost blank page. The narration
on the next page describes Tayo, the main character, waking up to the
sunlight on the wall of his room. The last words of the novel repeat this
effect and offer a marvelous image for the implications of the words.
Sunrises speak of liminality, of thresholds to be crossed. Time passes, and
creation begins again with daybreak.

Reading *Ceremony*

Reading *Ceremony* is in many ways an exercise in frustration, especially
for nonnative readers. The novel replicates Tayo's confusion and disorientation in the reader by constantly shifting scenes, settings, and form.
The frustration that this may produce is, however, a prominent feature
in the beauty and power of the novel. The reader experiences in a small
way what Tayo has to overcome, and readers who complete the ritual of
reading are left with a vision of the world not unlike that of Tayo's at the
end. This is a vision that heals deep wounds and provides hope in the
possibility of creation rather than fear at the realities of destruction.

The structure and style of the novel also frustrate attempts to produce traditional criticism of it. Much more than a shattered narrative
line, this novel is a spiderweb of interconnecting stories, themes, and
events, and any attempt to straighten out these lines is bound to fail, to
break the web. Most of the interpretations of the novel, then, tend to
follow one or two strands, such as women or stories, and leave the rest
for others. This is a useful approach and helps us to see parts of the pattern more clearly. *Ceremony,* however, is read in time without the benefit
of seeing these strands at the beginning, and this is precisely the situa-

tion in which Tayo finds himself initially. The reader's experience in *Ceremony*, then, should also be taken into account. Although this is a noble goal, reflecting that experience in a book like this one is difficult. The following pages attempt to account for the experience of reading *Ceremony* as it comes at readers on the page. The result will reflect the structure of the novel itself, showing the fragmentation and disorientation that are part of Tayo's experience. I conclude this chapter by tracing three particular elements of the web: women, language, and identity.

The opening poem sets the stage for the most important aspects of the novel.[2] Here we learn from at least two nameless voices about the significance of stories and ceremonies. The first line introduces readers to Ts'its'tsi'nako, Thought-Woman, who is sitting in her room thinking of a story. She thinks of her sisters, who with her created the universe, or the five worlds.[3] Thought-Woman is also the spider, the grandmother creatrix found in much of southwestern mythology. Spider-Woman is the mother of the twins, who are the culture heroes of the Pueblo people. A first-person voice informs us that she is telling the same story that Spider-Woman is thinking. Then another voice enters the dialogue. This voice is male and speaks about the power of stories, reminding us that they are not just entertainment; rather, they are "all we have to fight off / illness and death. / You don't have anything if you don't have the stories." There is evil in the world, but it cannot overwhelm a story. "He rubbed his belly. / I keep them here" is an important line in this opening poem. It indicates the place where stories reside, which is not, as Westerners might imagine, in the head but in the belly, where they provide sustenance and life. This voice invites his audience to touch his belly so that we can feel that "it is moving. / There is life here / for the people." That life is growing just as "the belly of this story" is growing. Stories are like people; they conceive and nurture other stories. The next page is blank except for a few lines at the bottom that reply to the male voice. The lines begin with the italicized "What She Said," and what she said is that the only cure she knows is a good ceremony. The next page has only one word near the top—Sunrise—and the following page begins the prose narration but starts low on the page with only six lines at the bottom. This is the sunrise effect discussed earlier.

The beginning of the novel does not offer a coherent vision of the world. On the contrary, readers begin the prose portion of the novel by entering Tayo's tortured mind. He is just beginning to awaken, and in that state between consciousness and unconsciousness, he experiences a cacophony of voices and a kaleidoscope of images. "Tayo didn't sleep well that night" are the first words after the poem. The night had been one of "humid dreams" and voices that "rolled him over and over again like debris caught in a flood." The voices are Spanish—a man singing a familiar love song, Japanese—angry and loud voices of soldiers, and Laguna—the voice of his Uncle Josiah bringing him fever medicine. He also thinks he hears his mother's voice but cannot understand the words. Finally, all the voices are drowned out by the sound of a jukebox, "its flashing red and blue lights pulling the darkness closer." As Tayo stares at the small rectangle of the sunrise on the wall made by a high, small window, he reflects on the fact that he had not been able to sleep for a long time. Tayo's problem is not that he experiences such memories; rather, his difficulty is that these memories are not isolated at all. Instead they are "tied together like colts in single file." The only solution Tayo has to his acute problems is to try to imagine something completely unconnected, something not tied to anything else.

> So Tayo had to sweat through those nights when thoughts became entangled; he had to sweat to think of something that wasn't unraveled or tied in knots to the past—something that existed by itself, standing alone like a deer. And if he could hold that image of the deer in his mind long enough, his stomach might shiver less and let him sleep for a while. It worked as long as the deer was alone, as long as he could keep it a gray buck on an unrecognized hill; but if he did not hold it tight, it would spin away from him and become the deer he and Rocky had hunted. (7)

Tayo is sick because he cannot see the pattern. He observes all the elements only too well, but there is no apparent narrative that will bring the elements of his life together in a meaningful way. Approximately the first third of the novel replicates Tayo's confusion in the reader by frequently shifting scenes, perspectives, and time sequences. The result is that readers become disoriented in the world of the story and yearn for some sort of narrative structure that will indicate the way. We readers want a ceremony ourselves. As James Ruppert notes, this is one of the reader's lessons in the novel.[4]

Tayo's sickness is a reflection of a much larger problem, specifically, a devastating drought in the Laguna area. This drought is clearly a result of Tayo's cursing of the rain when he was in the Philippines: "So he had prayed the rain away, and for the sixth year it was dry; the grass turned yellow and it did not grow. Wherever he looked, Tayo could see the consequences of his praying" (14). He and his cousin Rocky were taken prisoner by the Japanese and forced on the Bataan death march. Before they arrived at the prison camp, Rocky died as the rain came down. It was then that Tayo cursed the incessant rain that quickly buried Rocky's body in mud and water. The desiccated earth that appears in the beginning scenes of the novel is the effect of Tayo's curse. It is also a sign of mother earth's displeasure at her children's participation in a devastating world war, the second in the first part of the century. Tayo's nemesis, Emo, who has also just returned from the war, articulates the effects of the drought with an especially sharp edge: "Emo liked to point to the restless dusty wind and the cloudless skies, to the bony horses chewing on fence posts beside the highway; Emo liked to say, 'Look what is here for us, Look. Here's the Indians' mother earth! Old dried-up thing!' Tayo's anger made his hands shake. Emo was wrong. All wrong" (25).

Even here Tayo's problem of interpretation is reflected. He recognizes that something is wrong but is unwilling or unable to offer a coherent reason for the predicament. Having accepted the boundaries and identities drawn by white culture, Emo does not have this problem. He sees only what reinforces those values and assumptions about the world. Tayo, on the other hand, is a "radical reader" who rejects easy interpretations of the world, whether they are Laguna or Euro-American.[5] The inadequacy that Tayo sees in his interpretive options places him in a marginalized position between mythologies or ways of understanding the world and his place in it. His disorientation and physical illness are results of this spacelessness. The army psychiatrist tries to induct him into the rituals of American identity by using standard therapeutic techniques, and this works only enough for Tayo to be released from the army hospital. He makes it to the train station before passing out, only to wake up to see Japanese faces hovering above him. For a moment he thinks he is back in the war until someone explains to him that the conflict is over. Drifting in time and space and experiencing everything at once without any frame of reference, Tayo wants only to become smoke, to be unconnected like the deer he imagines on a "nameless hill." One of the most dramatic instances of this inability to disengage from the connectedness of things occurs when Tayo is told to shoot Japanese soldiers lined up in front of a cave. Tayo cannot pull the trigger because "in that instant he saw Josiah standing there." Tayo cannot be convinced that one of these soldiers is anything but his beloved uncle: "He *knew* it was Josiah; and even after Rocky started shaking him by the shoulders and telling him to stop crying, it was still Josiah lying there." Even after they roll the body over and Rocky shouts "This is a Jap!," Tayo begins screaming because he still sees Josiah's body. The combination of connectedness and interpretive chaos makes Tayo sick. His condition, especially after the psychiatrist fails him, calls to mind the female voice from the opening poem: "The only cure / I know / is a good ceremony, / that's what she said."

After we learn of Tayo's nightmarish experiences in the jungle, on the Bataan death march and in the prisoner-of-war camp, the second verse section of the novel appears. Just over a page long, this account describes the fighting between two sisters. They are in fact goddesses of Laguna mythology named Iktoa'ak'o'ya (Reed Woman) and Corn Woman. It was summertime, and Reed Woman spent all her time bathing, "sitting in the river / splashing down / the summer rain." Her sister Corn Woman works hard every day in the field sweating and getting sore hands. Finally, Corn Woman tires of her sister's behavior and expresses her anger by scolding her for bathing all day long. Reed Woman responds by leaving the fifth world and going back into the fourth world, "to the original place / down below." The next line reveals the connection to Tayo's story: "And there was no more rain then." Reed Woman's departure causes a drought, and people and animals are thirsty and starving because all the rain is gone and the corn and beans have dried up and blown away. This story parallels Tayo's attempt to set things right with himself and the world.

One of the symptoms of Tayo's illness is that he frequently vomits and urinates. The psychological implications of these symptoms are obvious: Tayo's body is trying to purge itself of some poison. Like everything else in this novel, however, the explanation is not that simple. Tayo's malady is a function of something much deeper, and the fact that the source of this pain is in his belly is significant. Tayo experiences "a swelling in his belly, a great swollen grief that was pushing into his throat"; the ultimate source of this grief remains unknown to the reader and Tayo until the latter part of the novel when Tayo nears the completion of his ceremony. To understand this illness, it is helpful to recall the opening poem's male voice, which says that he keeps his stories in his belly. Tayo's belly contains a sickness that he is trying to purge; a story would be a tonic to him. When the army psychiatrist asks Tayo why he cries, Tayo tells him that it is because "they are dead and everything is dying." When he goes on to tell Tayo that he can cry, Tayo gags as he tastes his own tears and curses at the doctor. Obviously, Tayo does not suffer from repression or any of the other disorders that the psychiatric profession can diagnose and treat. What he needs is a ceremony. Immediately after this conversation with the doctor, Tayo passes out at the train station after a Japanese woman and child ask if he is okay. Upon coming out of his fainting spell, he suffers more nausea as the swelling continues to push against his throat. He vomits into the garbage can, and when he can vomit no more, he begins to cry: "He cried at how the world had come undone, how thousands of miles, high ocean waves and green jungles could not hold people in their place."

Somewhere in the kaleidoscope of his memories, Tayo knows the cure he needs. Remembering times when he and his cousin Rocky wandered the mesas and valleys, he recalls: "Distances and days existed in themselves then; they all had a story. They were not barriers. If a person wanted to get to the moon, there was a way; it all depended on whether you knew the story of how others before you had gone. He had believed in the stories for a long time, until the teachers at Indian school taught him not to believe in that kind of 'nonsense.' But they had been wrong. Josiah had been there, in the jungle; he had come. Tayo had watched him die, and he had done nothing to save him" (19). Back home at Laguna with Auntie and Old Grandma, Tayo does not find the story he needs. Auntie is a bitter and jealous woman who is more concerned with her status among her Catholic friends than with helping her sister's son. She blames Tayo for allowing Rocky to die and thinks that Tayo should have been the one to perish, given the moral consequences espoused by her adopted Christianity. Grandma is kinder and more in touch with the old ways. As Tayo gets sicker and sicker in his boyhood home, he desires more and more to return to the army hospital where he can disconnect from the world and become white smoke. Grandma realizes that the white medicine has not helped him at all and calls for the tribal medicine man. Displeased with this development, Auntie worries about the appropriateness of calling in a medicine man for a half-breed like Tayo, and doing so is sure to start the stories of Tayo's mother, Laura, sleeping with whites and Mexicans. There is also her brother Josiah's scandalous encounter with a Mexican woman from Cubero who is fodder for the gossipmongers. Grandma, however, is adamant about Tayo needing help from tribal medicine and tells Auntie that any gossip that is started from this encounter will be forgotten by planting time. Auntie reminds Grandma that the army doctor has expressly forbidden Tayo to receive any Indian medicine. This clash between Grandma and Auntie depicts an important theme in the novel, namely, the nature of time. Grandma, more attuned to the vagaries of time and circumstance reflected in the stories, realizes that things change, that with planting comes a new time. Auntie, on the other hand, operating as she does with her Christian sense of time, understands the world in terms that do not recognize the passage of time. For her, things done once are done for all, and no forgiveness is available unless there is a wiping away of those sins in the act of conversion. Time and change are two aspects of life that Tayo must come to grips with before he can be healed. Did he kill Josiah? Did he cause the drought? Does he need forgiveness, or does he need a ceremony that will wrap a story around his experience?

Grandma succeeds in arranging for a visit from the tribal medicine man. Old Ku'oosh visits Tayo on his sickbed and tells him of a cave nearby. Tayo is embarrassed at first because Ku'oosh's words sound childish and are interspersed with English, but then he begins to remember the cave. Snakes used to lie at its mouth to restore life to themselves. The story in the old days was that people would throw scalps down into the cave. When Tayo looks confused, Ku'oosh acknowledges Tayo's white father and indicates that that is the reason Tayo does not understand the importance of language and story. Ku'oosh remarks that the world is fragile, and the way he says it implies that the world is made of stories, stories that have the nature of spider webs, strong but always needing to be rewoven. In fact, Ku'oosh indicates that the responsibility of being human is knowing and telling the story behind each word so that there can be no mistake as to the meaning. Such an understanding of words and humanity demands great patience and love.

Ku'oosh then asks Tayo a most important question for his ceremony: Did he kill anyone in the war? Tayo frankly cannot remember whether he did or not. All he knows is that he has done something far worse than kill an enemy: He has cursed the earth, and the effects of that are everywhere. After vomiting again, Tayo turns shivering and sweating to the old man and tells him that, to his knowledge, he has never killed anyone. Ku'oosh simply shakes his head. He cannot imagine warfare where enemies can kill each other without knowing it. Tayo believes that even if he could take the old man to the battlefield and show him the craters and corpses, he would not believe what had happened. He would say that something close and monstrous had killed those people because "not even oldtime witches killed like that."

After this episode with the medicine man, Silko inserts another Laguna poem. The poem deals with "the old days / long time ago" when there was a Scalp Society. Membership in this group was limited to those who had killed or touched dead enemies. These warriors were haunted by K'oo'ko, a demoness with great fangs who threatens the earth and its creatures. The poem indicates that one of the dangers involved in torture and killing is that the rain would not come. There are things the warriors must do to correct the situation, ceremonies to perform to rectify the imbalance in the world. It is interesting that Silko would include this story, which explains why Ku'oosh is asking Tayo about his actions in the war, and that may be reason enough for including it. At the same time, the reader knows better than to think that this is Tayo's problem. From the first few pages we know that killing is not what wrecked Tayo's health. We know also that Tayo refused to kill when asked because all he could see was Uncle Josiah instead of the Japanese soldiers. In a novel where the reader is constantly being challenged to "see the pattern," perhaps this inside information helps us to comprehend that Ku'oosh's ceremony is not going to work. Indeed, the ceremony is only partial, and although it stops Tayo's physical symptoms of vomiting and urinating, it is clearly not the ceremony he needs to be fully healed. Ku'oosh admits as much when he says to Tayo, "There are some things we can't cure like we used to . . . not since the white people came." He goes on to tell him that his ceremony has failed to help some of the others who also returned from the war sick. What the ceremony does do is convince Tayo of something he suspected all along: that his own destructive power is greater than he imagined. It takes only one person to tear away the delicate web that holds the world together.

Leroy, Emo, and Harley stand in contrast to Tayo in their reactions and adjustments to coming home from the war. Harley and Leroy are typical of many Native American veterans in their ability to slip back into the notions of being Indian that had been temporarily suspended during the war.[6] Tayo and Emo are not so easily cast in this role, yet they are markedly different in their attitudes. We have already seen that Emo has given up on mother earth and considers her an old, dried-up thing, a carcass left over from the long-lost battle with the whites. Tayo knows deep down that Emo is wrong, but he cannot see why exactly. Of these war buddies returned home, Harley is the closest friend Tayo has, and Emo is his enemy. Despite these complex and conflicting emotions, they all end up together at various times in the novel and with intriguing results. Their common ritual is to meet at a bar when their government checks come in and spend their time drinking and telling stories about the war. Invariably involving the conquest of white women, these stories describe men using their ethnicity to seduce the women. For Tayo, alcohol is a kind of medicine: "Liquor was medicine for the anger that made them hurt, for the pain of the loss, medicine for tight bellies and choked-up throats. He was beginning to feel a comfortable place inside himself, close to his own beating heart, near his own warm belly; he crawled inside and watched the storm swirling on the outside and he was safe there; the winds of rage could not touch him" (40).

When Tayo is urged to tell a story, he gives them the only one he knows, the only one he can see that is real: "One time there were these Indians, see," he begins. They cut their hair, put on uniforms, and went off to war. They were treated the same as whites: They got alcohol, smiles, and sex as much as they wanted. They also got the "same medals for bravery, the same flag over the coffin." Tayo's story does not entertain the veterans the way their own do. No one laughs, and they look at him in stunned silence. Tayo is telling the real story and will not let the jukebox or anything stop him from completing it. He goes on to explain that the dumb Indians expected this situation to last, but it did not. The similarity, the level playing field, the absence of institutional racism was suspended because there was another target for the machinations of difference, and that was the enemy, the Japanese. Once that scapegoat was taken care of, the old hierarchies of racism returned. Tayo has now worked himself into a state: "Goddamn it! You stupid sonofabitches! You know!" They do indeed know that what Tayo says is true, only they are unwilling to acknowledge it, unwilling to change the ceremony to fit the new situation. Although Tayo does not know the new ceremony, he does know that the old one is obsolete because things in the world have shifted. As the men carefully begin telling the stories of the war to erase Tayo's story from their minds, Tayo begins to cry. He cries for them repeating these stories "like long medicine chants, the beer bottles pounding on the counter tops like drums." This is their ceremony: telling stories of the past that have no relevance to the present while pounding out cadences with the empty containers of their poison.

The next verse section of the novel begins the longest of the interwoven Laguna stories and most closely parallels Tayo's own journey. This is the story of the arrival of Pa'caya'nyi, a magician from Reedleaf town up north. When Pa'caya'nyi asks the people if they would like to learn some magic, they reply that they can always use some. The twins Ma'see'wi and Ou'yu'ye'wi were caring for the mother corn altar but become interested in this new magic.[7] After the magician performs a few tricks, the twins are impressed and begin to play around with this Ck'o'yo magic instead of caring for the corn altar. They assume that the magic will provide a new source of life and that corn and animals can be created with it, but "they didn't know it was all just a trick." The mother gets very angry and says to herself, "If they like that magic so much / let them live off it," and then she takes the plants and grass from them. No baby animals are born, and the rainclouds disappear. The resemblance to Tayo's situation is obvious, especially given the representation of the other veterans and their ceremonies. The "benefits" of the war are transitory and illusory because they are made of nothing; it is all just a trick. Sustenance for physical and emotional life comes not from money or people who have power but from the source of life, the earth. By running the veterans' stories alongside the Laguna stories, Silko shows us that a contemporary story can lack continuity and relevance, whereas an ancient story can have both.

After the verse story of the Ck'o'yo medicine man and his seduction of the people by magic, we journey back in time to a hunt when Tayo and Rocky killed a deer. We learn of Rocky's successful assimilation into white culture and Tayo's ambivalence about it all. Upon finding the deer dying in the grass, Tayo wants to touch it and recalls wanting to pet a deer as long as he can remember. For him it is a sacred moment just before life passes from its eyes, and "he knew what they said about deer was true." This is most likely the belief that deer come down from the mountains to offer themselves to the Laguna hunters. The hunters are to be grateful and thank the deer for this act, otherwise the deer will not return to be killed next year.[8] Even though he is full-blooded, Rocky does not see the deer as sacred. When Tayo covers the head before Rocky guts it, Rocky asks why, even though they both know why. Rocky has garnered the accolades and trophies of assimilation. An A student and an all-state athlete, he knows how to win. Moreover, he listens to the white authority figures who plot his life and tell him that the only thing that can hold him back is the Laguna community. Grandma shakes her head when he opens his textbooks to show her that the Laguna way is mere superstition. Auntie, however, encourages his assimilation because it will help to negate the gossip about her own sister and Tayo. The deer, or the interpretation of the death of the deer, becomes a contested site for two very different ways of seeing the world.

The connections between Emo, Rocky, and Tayo are thrown into relief by the story of the magician who seduces the people. The story serves to show that the old stories are not in fact obsolete but entirely relevant to contemporary events. In fact, the stories exist in spite of people's ignorance of them. This fact is illustrated dramatically by the following pages of prose and the verse sections within them. From the recollection of the killing of the deer, the scene moves back to the bar where Tayo and the war veterans are drinking away their army paycheck. Tayo is disturbingly silent, and Harley is worried that Tayo may become violent as he did once before. There is talk of an incident when Tayo attacked Emo, and they discuss the interpretation of that event. Tayo suggests that he was crazy, but Harley rejects that explanation by claiming that Tayo was simply drunk. The army doctor seems to agree with Harley somewhat and reads Tayo reports of alcohol-related violence among Native American veterans.[9]

Just after these descriptions, Silko includes another part of the story begun earlier in verse form. In fact, it picks up as if we had just read the previous line of the story, and in some ways we have. The people determine that the drought is caused by the corn mother, who is angry at them for playing around with magic. They notice that hummingbird is not suffering at all, and he tells them that in the worlds below everything is verdant and fruitful, so he goes down there to eat. The implications of this part of the story are significant. There is a source of life unaffected by magic. Where the mother is, there are life and health. Where the crisis is resolved, there exists an order that remains apart from the current crisis. This is one of the most important stories of *Ceremony;* namely, in creation there is hope in spite of the power of destruction. This theme sets *Ceremony* apart from *House Made of Dawn,* for example, which offers little sense of optimism as Abel races to his death at the end. Tayo is looking for life, and because we know that life exists in the worlds below, we have hope for Tayo that he can find the source. Tayo is confident, too; he knows the stories are powerful. What he needs is a ceremony, a story that is acted out, that will reorient him. Later on, when he sees a hummingbird, he thinks, "as long as the hummingbird had not abandoned the land, somewhere there were still flowers, and they could all go on."

The prose section picks back up with Harley reminding Tayo that he was lucky not to be sent to jail for attacking Emo and then immediately shifts to the same bar but just before Tayo's attack. Here Emo is playing with a bag of teeth that he has knocked out of the mouth of a dead Japanese officer. He treats the bag of teeth like a fetish, an object of sacred power, so it is not surprising that he wraps his actions in a story. He begins by claiming that they deserve better than "this goddamn dried-up country around here." His other sentences rhyme, and he laughs at this, but it also cues the reader that ritual language is at work, such as in a chant. Emo declaims that in the imaginary world where

Indians rule, he will take San Diego and that they all deserve more because they fought the war for the whites, but the whites possess everything. As Emo rants, the others chime in with statements of affirmation at appropriate points in the diatribe; clearly a community is being formed out of bitterness and desire. Tayo, however, does not participate. He sits, quietly clenching his muscles against the tirade and thinking of a tumbling cold stream. Finally realizing that Tayo is breaking the circle, Emo castigates him publicly. Tayo walks into the bathroom and urinates a clear stream. When he returns, Emo is ready for him and calls him a half-breed.

At this point, another verse story "interrupts" the novel, but this poem is different from the rest. Although it appears in the same form as the other Laguna stories, the content is supplied by Emo. This is the story of Emo's conquest of white women. He does this by appropriating different ethnic identities in his hunt for women in bars. On the night described in the poem, he decides to be Italian and tells the women his name is Mattuci, a member of his unit. Emo seduces two women that night and ends the story with a joke that he is making some reputation for Mattuci. The men laugh and tell Emo that that was a good one. Tayo simply stares at him, and Emo correctly surmises that Tayo does not like his stories. When Tayo does not respond, the ritual of the teeth in the bag begins again. Now the stories turn to killing, and Emo recounts with pride the story of the teeth, how they came from a Japanese colonel. Tayo sees how Emo grows from the killing and from the telling of it. Finally, something snaps, and Tayo crushes the beer bottle in his hands and plunges the broken edges into Emo's belly. As he watches Emo jerk, Tayo begins to feel stronger and believes that he can get well if he kills him. This is, of course, a ratification of Emo's story and ritual, that killing heals and makes one stronger. Tayo experiences this release as well, noting that "the space to carry hate was . . . empty."

By attacking Emo, Tayo is succumbing to the power of Emo's story and living it out. Although this offers some relief for Tayo's twisted stomach that holds the hate, it is ultimately destructive. Tayo's attack is analogous to his body's attempt to purge itself through vomiting and urinating. Such actions are not cures but symptoms, and even though Tayo feels better just after the attack, even he knows that the illness from which he suffers is chronic. Allowing the symptoms to overcome him only makes him sicker in the end. In terms of larger symbolic patterns, Tayo's actions place him squarely in the company of those stories and rituals of killing that he despises and that made him angry in the first place, especially those stories connected with military service. Accordingly, Silko offers an account of how Tayo and Rocky were recruited into the army. "Anyone can fight for America," says the recruiter as he offers Tayo and Rocky a promise of becoming true Americans by participating in one of its institutions for ritual killing. Rocky sees joining up as an initiation ritual into full citizenship that will enable them to travel around the world and perhaps have a government car. After the recruiter signs them up, Tayo immediately regrets his action because he realizes that he has broken his promise to help out with the garden and the sheep camp.

To illustrate this double pull upon Tayo's allegiances and perhaps to foreshadow how his new army family will fail him, Silko embeds the story of Tayo's abandonment within the recruitment story. At the age of four, Tayo was left with Josiah and Auntie, and Auntie comes to despise him privately while publicly pretending to adopt him. She even refuses to let Tayo play in another room alone; she wants him to see how much she loves Rocky: "She wanted him close enough to feel excluded, to be aware of the distance between them" (67). Tayo lives with this duplicity much better than Auntie does, and Tayo conjectures that Auntie understands him better than the others because of it. Even in his disorientation and interpretive confusion, Tayo is able to see that Auntie's duplicity is a result of the colonization of native life and land, which has "become entangled with European names," and that "the people would have no rest until the entanglement had been unwound to the source." Auntie is a Christian, and "Christianity separated the people from themselves." So Tayo and Auntie are alike in at least one important way: They both have been split in two by the coexistence of European and native ideologies. Whereas Tayo tries to put them both into some kind of pattern, Auntie tries to assimilate and thereby to ignore the native worldview that she has inherited, a worldview that now is obsolete to those who she believes are important.

Subtly but deftly the narrative then moves into one of the few sections that offer information on Tayo's mother, Laura, who is Auntie's little sister. The trouble began when Laura started drinking and running around with white and Mexican men. The Catholic priest is upset at the drunkenness and lust, but her relatives in the pueblo know that the problem runs much deeper: "[T]hey were losing her, they were losing a part of themselves." Just as the army recruiter offers Tayo and Rocky a family away from home, Laura's missionary teachers had "urged her to break away from her home," and for a while she relishes her new identity and enjoys the looks she gets from white men and from the reflection of herself in the street windows. After being with them, however, she "could feel the truth in their fists and in their greedy feeble lovemaking." This truth is the same one that Tayo learns when he returns from service: In Euro-American culture, difference cannot be overcome by love or war; the structures that define native and white are stronger than human emotion and national rituals.

Even though it is tempting to see Tayo's mother as a victim, that is not the only interpretation that can be offered. As the narrative moves back to Auntie's perspective, we learn that she confides in Tayo about one incident involving his mother that she has told no one else about. One morning around sunrise, Auntie went for a walk down by the river and discovered Laura coming down a trail on the other side. Tayo's mother is naked except for her high heel shoes, and she drops her purse under an old cottonwood tree. Auntie tells Tayo this because he "has to understand." As we shall see in *Storyteller,* the river, cottonwoods, a trail on other side of the river, and a woman walking are all components of the Yellow Woman stories from Laguna mythology. Yellow Woman is not a victim, although she can suffer and even be killed. She exemplifies the dangers and rewards of exploring relationships, of tying the world together rather than splitting it apart. She represents what Tayo is after, namely, a coherent vision of the world that does not categorize; instead, it weaves in order to incorporate everything. His mother is a Yellow Woman, and like some of her mythological predecessors, she does not return. She is the absent mother of the novel and the absent center that Tayo seeks. Like Yellow Woman, she also represents mother earth and the creative power she holds within. In the middle of the prose section where Auntie is telling Tayo this story, Silko inserts the next episode in the long poem about the attempt to recover from the witchery. Previously, the corn mother has withdrawn to the fourth world because of the neglect of her altar. The story picks up with the people saying "So that's where our mother went." The implications here are that Tayo's mother is like the corn mother who went away, and Tayo's search for healing is in some way a search for his own mother. After the poem, Silko brings us back to the story of Tayo and Rocky joining the army. The setting is an argument among the "family" over whether Tayo should go with Rocky. It ends with Tayo telling Grandma "I'll bring him back safe."

This section of the novel is significant in terms of the reader's development and understanding of Tayo's cure. By telescoping the narrative into a tighter and tighter focus, Silko alerts us to the fact that there is an

absent mother in the story and that finding her is crucial to the completion of the ceremony. From here on, the narrative proceeds to a section
on the speckled cattle that are bred for life in the New Mexican desert
but whose disappearance figures into Tayo's ceremony, for he will have
to recover them when they run away. This is followed by a reflection
upon Josiah's encounter with the Night Swan, another Yellow Woman
figure who is also a part of Tayo's ceremony through memory. The
Night Swan tells Tayo to remember their encounter because he will recognize it later. He does recognize it, and so do we when he encounters
other mountain women who represent the absent mother, who is, of
course, ultimately the earth herself, and these women represent her.
After this section, women begin to emerge more frequently from both
the past and the present, and with these appearances come broader perspectives for Tayo and the reader. Tayo recalls a visit to Dripping Springs
before he went off to war. While there, he had a vision of the pattern
that he was to lose during the war: "Everywhere he looked, he saw a
world made of stories, the long ago, time immemorial stories, as old
Grandma called them. It was a world alive, always changing and moving; and if you knew where to look, you could see it, sometimes almost
imperceptible, like the motion of the stars across the sky" (95). As
women begin to appear more frequently and with greater importance,
the rhythm of the novel changes and the stories become longer and
wider in scope. The ceremony has begun, the pattern starts to emerge,
and Tayo's vision has begun to focus.

After another episode in the poem describes the finding of the
mother, who says that a ceremony must be performed before she will
return the rain, Tayo meets the person who will supplement Ku'oosh's
ceremony with one that is less traditional but more effective. This is
Betonie, a Navajo who lives above Gallup and uses fetishes from both
native and white culture to perform his ceremonies. Among the materials from white culture are calendars and telephone books because "all
these things have stories in them." Betonie confirms that Tayo has
already initiated the ceremony he needs to become whole again; he has
simply come to an important place in the story, and the implication is
that we as readers have as well. Instead of reeling to and fro as Tayo does
when he is sick, the story world begins to stabilize, and we settle down
into longer narrative sections and begin to discern a plot. Betonie represents this effect nicely by offering explanations for things. One of the
first pieces that Betonie fits into the puzzle concerns Tayo's refusal to
shoot Japanese soldiers during the war: " 'The Japanese,' the medicine

man went on, as though he were trying to remember something. 'It isn't surprising you saw him with them. You saw who they were. Thirty thousand years ago they were not strangers. You saw what the evil had done: you saw the witchery ranging as wide as this world' " (124). Betonie's methods are unorthodox, but that is precisely the point: The world has changed and needs new ceremonies that reflect the changes. He explains that "after the white people came, elements in this world began to shift; and it became necessary to create new ceremonies." These new ceremonies engender suspicion in the traditionals but reflect the growth of the rituals that matches the growth of the world. One of the issues most distressing to colonized native cultures—other than the obvious elements of murder and theft—was the degree to which the world changed in a short period of time. The reaction that Ku'oosh has at hearing that a killing can occur without the knowledge of the killer is one example of this rapid change. Such a concept is unthinkable to him but has become commonplace for Emo and his compatriots. What is called for is a fundamental change in the ceremonies that will keep apace with the changes, for good or ill, in the human race.

Even though the ceremonies must change, the realities conveyed by them do not, at least for Betonie. He is at heart a traditional. For example, he uses the material culture of white civilization but does not adopt their notions of difference and polarity. "Don't be so quick to call something good or bad," he tells Tayo. Those are the colonizers' terms. Betonie sees the world as a collection of balances and harmonies that are always in flux but always maintained. He likens the process to caring for a seedling: One makes adjustments for drought or excessive rain, but the sun and the rain are neither good nor evil. It is the balance that matters. With Betonie's help, Tayo is initiated into the type of relation that the army psychiatrist cannot even imagine, but his mother can.

The ceremony proper is a Navajo sandpainting ritual where the suffering one is placed in the center and a pattern is drawn around the sufferer that represents the journey back to the individual's origins and forward to his or her healing. There are several stages in the ceremony, but the ending has special meaning. Betonie chants on behalf of Tayo: "I'm walking back to belonging / I'm walking home to happiness / I'm walking back to long life" (144). Then they spin him around "sunwise / and he recovered." The text is clear, however, about the limits of this ceremony; there is a larger rite to perform because "all kinds of evil were still on him." Having completed the ritual that initiates him into the larger ceremony, Tayo begins to see and feel better. Boundaries disappear and identities begin to merge: "He took a deep breath of cold mountain air: there were no boundaries; the world below and the sand paintings inside became the same that night. The mountains from all the directions had been gathered there that night" (145).

Now on a quest, Tayo meets interesting and dangerous people along the way. Yellow Women abound. Betonie tells Tayo a Yellow Woman story of his own, and later Tayo meets Helen Jean, a woman who is riding with Harley and Leroy. Also, Tayo's stomach is healed. Ku'oosh's ceremony helped to settle it, but with Betonie's ceremony, Tayo can no longer drink. After drinking several beers with his friends and Helen Jean, he vomits everything up. What before the ceremony was his medicine has now become his poison. After the beer is regurgitated, "all his past, all his life" keeps coming up as he holds his belly by the side of the road.

It is not surprising that Tayo heads home; that is one of the functions of the ceremony: The participant must start over. Tayo must also find Josiah's speckled cattle, and home is the place to start. On the way to Laguna, however, he is stopped by a woman who appears from nowhere. This is yet another Yellow Woman, and this one asks the provocative and double-edged question, "What are you doing here?" She offers him food, shelter, and love. After they make love, he rolls over on his back, and "under his leg he could feel the damp wide leaf pattern that had soaked into the blanket where she lay" (181). This sentence echoes the first line of Silko's "Yellow Woman": "My thigh clung with his dampness" (ST, 54). Here Tayo is the wandering one, and Yellow Woman is the abductor. She offers him a reconciliation with the earth, which she represents. The descriptions of their love-making are evocative of merging into the earth as Riverwoman does in the poem "When Sun Came to Riverwoman" (LW, 6).

As the pattern begins to show itself for both Tayo and the reader, Tayo finds himself on the trail of the cattle. One of the important functions of ritual is to create sacred time. Tayo finally feels it:

> The anticipation of what he might find was strung tight in his belly; suddenly the tension snapped and hurled him into the empty room where the ticking of the clock behind the curtains had ceased. He stopped the mare. The silence was inside, in his belly; there was no longer any hurry. The ride into the mountain had branched into all directions of time. He knew then why the oldtimers could only speak of yesterday and tomorrow in terms of the present moment: the only certainty; and this present sense of being was qualified with bare hints of yesterday or tomorrow by saying, "I go up to the mountain yesterday or I go up to the mountain

tomorrow." The ck'o'yo Kaup'a'ta somewhere is stacking his gambling sticks and waiting for a visitor; Rocky and I are walking across a ridge in the moonlight; Josiah and Robert are waiting for us. This night is a single night; and there has never been any other. (192)

Whereas Tayo was initially assaulted by a multitude of elements that would not come together in any sort of pattern, now the boundaries of time and space collapse, and his vision is clear: "Gathering the spotted cattle was only one color of sand falling from the fingertips; the design was still growing, but already long ago it had encircled him" (196).

There is yet another meeting with Yellow Woman for Tayo, and this time her name is Ts'eh. (Actually, that is her nickname because her Indian name is too long.) This is a reference to Ts'its'tse'nako, Thought-Woman, and also to Tse'pina, Mt. Taylor. She tells Tayo that she is a Montano but that he can call her Ts'eh. They make love and learn about the secret springs and flowers of the mountain. It would be easy for Silko to leave the story here, but there is more. As the characters in the verse sections of the novel say about the effort to bring back rain, "It isn't easy." Tayo has more to do, but "it's almost completed," she says, "we are coming to the end soon" (233). Much to his disappointment, she leaves him, but before she goes she tells him to remember everything.

Tayo finds himself at an abandoned uranium mine, and suddenly the pattern is in full view. He is at the center of the witchery of destruction. Betonie's chant during the sandpainting ceremony indicated that Tayo would have to go "[t]o the place / where whirling darkness started its journey" (142). This is that place. Trinity Site is where the first atomic bomb was exploded; it is three hundred miles southeast of the mine. The top secret laboratories are deep in the Jemez mountains, and Los Alamos is only a hundred miles northeast. The witchery, like the creation, "knew no boundaries." Tayo arrives at the convergence of the fate of the earth and all living things. Here "human beings were one clan again, united by the fate the destroyers planned for all of them." Despite the horror of this realization, Tayo is relieved because he sees that he was not insane: "He cried the relief he felt at finally seeing the pattern, the way all the stories fit together—the old stories, the war stories, their stories—to become the story that was still being told. He was not crazy; he had never been crazy. He had only seen and heard the world as it always was: no boundaries, only transitions through all distances and time" (246).

Again, the novel could have ended here, but Silko puts Tayo through one more test. The power of the witchery is strong—strong enough to

force Tayo to participate in it by joining the army and trying to kill
Emo. Emo reappears just as Tayo is seeing the pattern, and this time he
has a victim. Harley, Tayo's best friend, has been systematically tortured
by Emo. Portions of his body have been cut off and are being held in a
bloody paper bag. Emo is drunk and calls out to Tayo to look at his
buddy. Tayo is mesmerized and falls under the spell himself. He imagines taking the screwdriver in his pocket and driving it into Emo's skull.
The reader comes under the same spell and wants the horror to stop. We
want Tayo to relieve us of the pain by killing Emo. But to do so would
end the story according to the witches' ceremony: "[T]heir deadly ritual
for the autumn solstice would have been completed by him" (253). Tayo
resists because he can see the larger pattern. The stars, the final element
in the ceremony, tell him another story. They have always existed and
always will. They were there during the migration from the North, and
they will last beyond the fifth world. The story of the stars will go on;
killing will not change anything.

As the rain clouds gather on the horizon, Tayo returns to tell the old
ones the story. It takes him a long time because they ask about directions and landmarks and about the woman. Because he has seen her,
they will be blessed again. In the original manuscript of *Ceremony*, Silko
has Laura, Tayo's mother, return and gather with the family to hear the
story. In the final version, it is old grandmother who appears prominently. Her comment upon it all seems anticlimactic, humorous, and
profound all at the same time: "It seems like I already heard these stories before . . . only thing is, the names sound different" (260). The last
page of the novel is full of white space and echoes the beginning: "Sunrise, / accept this offering, / Sunrise." A new day has begun, the circle
has been completed, and the stories go on.

Women in *Ceremony*

I use the term *women* here because I think that it more accurately reflects
Silko's own understanding of what we may be inclined to term "the
feminine." Silko consistently embodies her ideas of the feminine in particular women, including female figures from Laguna Pueblo mythology
and the woman they call mother, namely, the earth.

Ironically, one of the ways Silko portrays women is through Tayo, an
alienated male. Readers of Native American literature will recognize this
trope in some of the best-known Native American novels such as N.
Scott Momaday's *House Made of Dawn* and James Welch's *Winter in the*

Blood. Tayo's curse has produced the drought in Laguna, a drought that not only serves to write his spiritual desiccation on the broadest canvas but also threatens Laguna communal life and represents mother earth's disfavor with her children who are engaged in a world war. Tayo's healing depends upon the degree to which he can reintegrate himself with the rhythms and stories of the earth, which are to be found in women.

Other men in the novel, specifically Tayo's war buddies, with whom he shares time and memory but nothing else, view women as an extension of the war, the same war that suddenly made them equal with their white comrades. White women are the ultimate conquest for Emo, Harley, and Leroy, and are even greater than the victories accomplished in the white man's war. Raving about the injustice of fighting the war and having nothing to show for it, Emo remarks, "They took our land, they took everything! So let's get our hands on white women!" As we have seen, at one point in the novel, their conquest stories are put into verse just as Silko has interspersed Laguna legends in this same form. It is as if to say that narratives of conquest turn upon women in the postwar life of these men. These stories become the myths they live by. Tayo seems to know that he cannot be healed by continued conquest; what he needs instead is to piece together the many shards of his existence.

Tayo is eventually cured through an elaborate ceremony that involves several women. The Night Swan appears before Tayo goes off to war but foreshadows the ceremony he will need afterward. The Night Swan is a lover of Tayo's beloved Uncle Josiah, and she mysteriously appears in Cubero, at the foot of Mount Taylor, and disappears after Josiah's death. Tayo goes to inform her that Josiah cannot make their appointment, and there and then she introduces him to mysteries of rain and love. The Night Swan is associated with the blue of Mount Taylor, which in Laguna is called Tse' pina or Woman Veiled in Rain Clouds. She is the blue of the mountain and synecdochically the blue of the west, of rain and wind. The rain envelops them as they make love, and the text reads: "She moved under him, her rhythm merging into the sound of the rain in the tree. And he was lost somewhere, deep beneath the surface of his own body and consciousness, swimming away from all his life before that hour" (99). They part in the midst of the smell of damp earth, and she says to Tayo, "You don't have to understand what is happening. But remember this day. You will recognize it later. You are a part of it now" (100).

Tayo does recognize this day later when he meets Ts'eh, a woman who lives on Mount Taylor. She is surrounded by the color yellow and thus is connected to the corn mother, pollen, and the Yellow Woman stories of Laguna mythology and lore that involve sacred and sexual abduction. Tayo is not physically abducted but does feel powerfully drawn to her. She feeds him corn the night before he rises to meet a dawn "spreading across the sky like yellow wings" (189). Like Yellow Woman, Ts'eh is both lover, mother, and mother earth as well. When Tayo dreams of making love with Ts'eh, the description indicates that he is being absorbed into the earth: "He felt the warm sand on his toes and knees; he felt her body, and it was warm as the sand, and he couldn't feel where her body ended and the sand began" (232).

Robert M. Nelson has pointed out that in *Ceremony* three dimensions of life, each reflecting the other, are affected by sickness or imbalance, namely, Tayo himself, Laguna society (as seen in Emo, Auntie, and others), and the earth.[10] Those three dimensions are brought into balance and focus by appropriate—that is, ritual—interaction with particular women. Paula Gunn Allen notes that there are two kinds of women in *Ceremony:* Tayo's mother, the Night Swan, and Ts'eh represent women who "belong to the earth spirit and live in harmony with her, even though this attunement may lead to tragedy," whereas Auntie symbolizes those "who are not of the earth but of human mechanism; they live to destroy that spirit, to enclose and enwrap it in their machinations, condemning all to a living death."[11] Tayo's healing comes about via ritualized encounters with the Night Swan and Ts'eh and perhaps also by understanding his mother's desertion of him through the themes of the Yellow Woman stories of Laguna mythology. Tayo, a man who is more at ease with other men like Rocky and Josiah than with women, recovers from the reeling vertigo of the "witchery" of war and white culture by losing his self to women. As I mentioned earlier, these encounters are ritualized, not merely sexual flings that act as an electroshock to Tayo's faltering ego. They are ceremonies of the earth and serve to center Tayo in the three areas in which there has been sickness: his own existence, Laguna culture and myth, and the earth itself.

Here, then, is a vision of women that shows them to embody the possibility of recovery, not of conquest. They are that to which one must return for healing and balance. At the same time, Silko does not present women as faultless goddesses. Auntie, who raised Tayo, is partly to blame for Tayo's illness since she is seduced, in Silko's words, by the witchery of destruction, the same witchery that brought white people and culture to Laguna. Such seduction is why women in *Ceremony* function as creators only in ritualized contexts, that is to say, when they are extensions of their mother, the earth. Women are not mere antidotes to the troubles of alienated men; rather, they are the source of life in balance for themselves and the world.

Women play a vital role in Tayo's ceremony. The encounter with the Night Swan foreshadows other ritualized encounters with women. Unlike his war buddies who see women as conquests of war, Tayo experiences love and sex with the mysterious mountain woman Ts'eh. Ts'eh is no doubt a shortened form of Ts'its'tsi'nako, or Thought-Woman, who begins the novel by thinking of a story. She appears in various forms but is always associated with Mount Taylor, which in Laguna is Tse'pina, or Woman Veiled in Rain Clouds. She is the spirit of Mount Taylor and an extension of the earth herself. She is the feminine principle embodied and thus is Yellow Woman, Corn Woman, and other female figures from Laguna mythology. When Tayo makes love to these different expressions of Thought Woman, he feels himself connected once again to a fertile and nurturing earth. He loses himself in the unity of all life and is no longer an invisible outcast; he has a place.

Language in *Ceremony*

It is easy to see the importance of women in this novel, but there is an equal significance given to language. In fact, the image of the web, Spider-Woman's web, appears throughout the novel. The spinning of the web is the spinning of tales, and these tales, if appropriately understood, can effect healing for individuals, society, and the earth. On the first page of the novel we read that the spider is thinking of a story, and we are told the story she is thinking. Further, the stories are "all we have to fight off illness and death." The tales connect everything in a web that is paradoxically both strong and fragile. When Ku'oosh first comes to offer a ceremony for Tayo, he remarks, "But you know, grandson, this world is fragile." The reader learns that the word *fragile* was "filled with the intricacies of a continuing process" and "with a strength inherent in spider webs." Tayo realizes that only one person, acting inappropriately, can tear away the delicate web and injure the world. These descriptions of storytelling as a web of words offer a profound explanation of the nature of language in oral cultures. Silko, in writing the novel, is continuing to spin the web.

The nature of language in Native American cultures is one of the most difficult elements for nonnatives to understand. Coming from a literate tradition that sees words as objects and from a print culture that sees books as "containing" meaning, it is difficult for Westerners to appreciate the dynamics of the oral tradition, a tradition that Silko and other Native American writers are self-consciously continuing. For many Native people, words are made of breath and thus have a life of their own. They come from the chest, which is near the heart, and thus are to be taken very seriously. Words are not symbols; they do not stand in between us and the object they represent. Words are the entities themselves in a different form. Paula Gunn Allen explains it this way: "The symbolism in American Indian ceremonial literature . . . is not symbolic in the usual sense; that is, the four mountains in the Mountain Chant do not stand for something else. They are those exact mountains perceived psychically, as it were, or mystically. The color red, as used by the Lakotas, doesn't stand for sacred or earth, but it is the quality of a being, the color of it, when perceived 'in a sacred manner' or from the point of view of the earth itself. That is, red is a psychic quality, not a material one, though it has a material dimension, of course. But its material aspect is not its essential one" (Allen, 69). Again she writes: "Symbols in American Indian systems are not symbolic in the usual sense of the word. The words articulate reality—not 'psychological' or imagined reality, not emotive reality captured metaphorically in an attempt to fuse thought and feeling, but that reality where thought and feeling are one, where objective and subjective are one, where speaker and listener are one, where sound and sense are one" (71).

One of the lessons of *Ceremony* is that language has power, the power to heal and the power to destroy. Language is not separable from its referents; on the contrary, it is the very stuff of story and thus the very stuff of life. In *The Delicacy and Strength of Lace,* Silko says she considers words to be analogous to the drawings in a sandpainting. They are the constellation we steer by, and, for Tayo, they provide him the orientation he needs to find his way home.

Identity in *Ceremony*

Tayo's problem does not center on assimilation into the white demarcations of difference and a loss of native understandings of wholeness as we might expect. Rather, his sickness comes from the inability to forget that wholeness when the world demands that he follow the dictates of colonial witchery. When Tayo is ordered to shoot Japanese soldiers, he is unable to follow this command because he sees his beloved Uncle Josiah's face in the place of the Japanese soldiers' faces. Even after Rocky turns over a Japanese corpse and forces Tayo to look into the eyes, all he can see is his uncle lying dead. For Tayo there is no *difference* between the soldiers and his uncle, and that lack of difference prevents Tayo from carrying out the orders he receives.

Later Tayo understands just why he could not appropriate the mind-set that was required to kill the soldiers. Betonie, a Navajo healer who uses contemporary repositories of information such as telephone books and calendars, tells Tayo that he saw the Japanese for what they are, namely, relatives of Native Americans. He remarks: "Thirty thousand years ago they were not strangers. You saw what the evil had done: you saw the witchery ranging as wide as this world" (124). Difference is the result of witchery; wholeness is the way things are.

The army psychiatrist who treats Tayo immediately after his return seeks to reinforce Tayo's individuality through difference. Tayo considers himself to be invisible, white smoke. The doctor sees Tayo's condition as pathological, but for Tayo his invisibility is a desperate attempt to integrate himself into the world of white culture. For Tayo, "[W]hite smoke had no consciousness of itself. It faded into the white world of their bed sheets and walls" (14). Tayo's psychiatric treatment is enforced by the introduction of difference to the degree that Tayo becomes separated from himself. The doctor's relentless questions batter him until the split is achieved and Tayo hears himself speaking to the doctor in the third person saying, "He can't talk to you. He is invisible. His words are formed with an invisible tongue, they have no sound" (15). Tayo ends this exchange between himself and the doctor by vomiting, a persistent symptom of his illness, and by proclaiming to the doctor, "Goddamn you, look what you have done" (16). The doctor has forced Tayo into distinctions of otherness and made those distinctions definitive. What he has not done is to provide Tayo with a story that can envelop those distinctions and hold them coherently so that the differences are not definitive or ultimate but fade into the larger perspective of the story. Such stories, writes Silko, have the strength and fragility of a spider's web. Tayo needs a ceremony of integration, not a dissertation on otherness and difference.

It is difficult to discuss identity in *Ceremony* without returning to the notions of language found there. Old Ku'oosh, the Laguna healer, knows about ceremonies and the strength and fragility of stories. When he first comes to Tayo, his instruction is on the nature of language. The medicine man speaks softly and with a dialect "full of sentences that were involuted with explanations of their own origins, as if nothing the old man said were his own but all had been said before and he was only there to repeat it" (34). The old man tells Tayo bluntly that this world is fragile:

> The word he chose to express "fragile" was filled with the intricacies of a continuing process, and with a strength inherent in spider webs woven across paths through sand hills where early in the morning the sun becomes entangled in each filament of web. It took a long time to explain the fragility and intricacy because no word exists alone, and the reason for choosing each word had to be explained with a story about why it must be said this certain way. That was the responsibility that went with being human, old Ku'oosh said, the story behind each word must be told so there could be no mistake in the meaning of what had been said; and this demanded great patience and love. (35–36)

Words are filaments in the web of stories, and all the stories are connected. This is their strength and their weakness, the strength and fragility of a spider web. Ku'oosh reminds Tayo that it takes only one person to tear away the delicate strands for the world to be injured. And Betonie confirms this idea for Tayo during his ceremony and reminds him that the ceremony is for the fragile world, not just for him.

Tayo's aunt knows the power of language both to ensnare and liberate. Language traps people into categories when used by the witchery of otherness but liberates people to be one with the stories when used creatively. Auntie lives with the knowledge of both. Tayo notices what he calls an old sensitivity that had descended in her, a sensitivity that derives from the time when the people shared a single clan name and "the same consciousness." With the coming of the witchery of white culture, the world is split in two. Everything suddenly has two names and, on the linguistic level, difference is created. Auntie accurately understands what has happened to Tayo when she remarks, "Christianity separated the people from themselves; it tried to crush the single clan name, encouraging each person to stand alone, because Jesus Christ would save only the individual soul" (68).

Tayo's soul cannot be separated from his body, or even from the body of the earth. His is not an individual salvation but includes the deliverance of the tribe and the earth. "You have seen her / We will be blessed again," say the old men when Tayo tells them of his healing. His journey is undertaken for everyone, and by resisting the witchery and embracing the mother, the world is set aright, the balances have shifted favorably, and the witchery is "dead for now." The novel ends with a new day beginning and an offering to the sun for the gift of life.

Ceremony stands as Silko's single greatest accomplishment as a writer. It is one of the most acclaimed novels written by a Native American and a foundational text for exploring the personal and cultural dimensions of America in the late twentieth century. Combining social criticism with mythical and ritual patterns, *Ceremony* offers readers a multitude of interpretive challenges and rewards. It is a signature novel for one of America's greatest storytellers.

Chapter Four
Storyteller: Spider-Woman's Web

If *Ceremony* challenges the genre of the novel, then *Storyteller* challenges the idea of the book.[1] An awkwardly bound compilation of photographs, mythology, gossip, short stories, and poetry, *Storyteller* enhances the uses of form to convey the dynamics of oral storytelling. The appearance of the book itself, with its elongated page-width, shorter page-length, and photographs, invites the interpretation that one is looking at a scrapbook or family album. Indeed, this is the case except on a much larger scale that involves Laguna history, animals, and the earth. There are stories of children, animals, and innocence as well as of adults, their creations, and the tragedies of experience. In spite of what seems on the surface to be a hodgepodge of genres and themes, *Storyteller* weaves itself into a spiderweb that brings together time, land, and experience and captures the essence of life and language in a way that diverse audiences can appreciate.

Storyteller is a unique showcase for Silko's work. It contains 25 poems, 16 of which do not appear in *Laguna Woman*. We also find the genre and the story that launched Silko's writing career, her short story "The Man to Send Rain Clouds." This is one of eight short stories in the book, including some of Silko's finest work, such as "Storyteller," "Lullaby," and "Yellow Woman."[2] There are also 26 black-and-white photographs, including 17 by Silko's father, Lee Marmon. The photographs are mostly of Silko's extended family from the early part of the century with a few landscape shots. There are also notes to the photographs that contain stories, not all of them related directly to the pictures. These photographs, like the other elements of the book, blend into the larger story like strands of a spiderweb. Between the poems, short stories, and photographs are interludes where Silko retells the stories she heard as a child and ruminates upon thoughts and incidents related to these stories. In all but the short stories, Silko uses her familiar device of line breaks, spacing, and white space to help convey the rhythm of oral storytelling.

Reading *Storyteller*

In many ways, reading *Storyteller* is the opposite of reading *Ceremony*. Rather than being confronted by the discordant notes of a cacophonous memory, the reader is presented with a childhood memory, still vivid and relished, of a large Hopi basket full of photographs. The connection reaches far back into the collective memory of the Laguna people and up to the present. The book itself is dedicated "to the storytellers / as far back as memory goes and to the telling / which continues and through which they all live / and we with them." Silko remarks on the first page: "It wasn't until I began this book / that I realized that the photographs in the Hopi basket / have a special relationship to the stories as I remember them. / The photographs are here because they are part of many of the stories / and because many of the stories can be traced in the photographs" (1). *Storyteller,* then, begins with the sacrament of memory, with the connections reaching far and wide, with the story already in place. The experience of reading the book is one of retracing collective memories of stories written upon the land and the body and carried in the minds of the people. Readers are privy to a ceremony where life, language, and land are celebrated as the boundaries of time dissolve in the service of a larger common identity.

There is a balance to the different genres in *Storyteller* that is assuring. The interludes in which Silko recollects or explains are not intrusive, just as the more crafted stories and poems blend into the larger picture without sharp edges. One way to explain this phenomenon is to say that the genre of autobiography lends itself to a more coherent reading experience. This may seem an odd claim, given the unusual structure of *Storyteller;* nevertheless, the book flows in ways that expose deeply personal dimensions of Silko's life while branching out into the larger dimensions of myth and history. The opening childhood memory sets a tone that is maintained throughout and implies that what is being read is not so much a story as a life—a life made of stories. Another reason for the seamlessness of the book is the simple fact that Tayo has such difficulty learning, namely, that all the stories are connected. *Storyteller* simply tells the stories, and they blend in fascinating ways. In a mythology class I taught recently, this was the favorite book by far. Students were amazed at (and grateful for) the ease with which they could see the connections. Some of them even mentioned that they were envious that they had no stories of their own and longed for the legacy left to Silko by her storytelling grandmothers and aunts. It should be pointed out that this is not

a children's book, although children may find much to enjoy in it. This
is a mature reflection upon identity, landscape, family, love, sex, and
power. That it occurs through the vehicle of family gossip, mythology
and lore, and images makes it all the more remarkable.

After the initial reflections upon the Hopi basket, the reader sees a
very old photograph of Robert G. Marmon and Marie Anaya (Grandmother A'mooh) holding an infant who is Silko's grandfather Hank.
The photograph is striking in its contrasts: the Union soldier and Presbyterian missionary with the huge mustache sits beside his wife and
looks to his left while Marie Anaya holds the child and looks in the
opposite direction. Hank is looking in the same direction as his father,
and Marie's dark hands stand out against the white of the baby's cloth-
ing and that of Robert's skin. This is the moment of the mixed blood, a
moment that will define Leslie Marmon Silko as a person and a writer.
Although the photograph could be of anyone's ancestors at the turn of
the century, a closer look shows that it has captured a historic moment
not only for Silko but for Laguna and even America.

On the next pages we learn of Aunt Susie, one of the formidable
women who helped to shape Silko's identity. Aunt Susie's personality
had been molded by Carlisle Indian School and Dickinson College in
Pennsylvania. She was a scholar who loved books and learning and listening to Leslie Marmon's childhood questions and speculations. She
was the last of a generation "that passed down an entire culture / by
word of mouth / an entire history / an entire vision of the world / which
depended upon memory / and retelling by subsequent generations" (6).
In the story of Aunt Susie, Silko finds her voice for the story of *Storyteller,*
for she writes, "As with any generation / the oral tradition depends upon
each person / listening and remembering a portion / and it is together—
/ all of us remembering what we have heard together— / that creates
the whole story / the long story of the people. / I remember only a small
part. / But this is what I remember" (7). Accompanying this remem-
brance of Aunt Susie is a photograph of her standing by a barbed-wire
fence looking down at the young Leslie Marmon. The story about Aunt
Susie sets the tone for the entire book. Readers know why the stories are
being told and why they are important. In these opening pages, Silko
also locates herself within the tradition she upholds. She has never over-
estimated her contribution to the storytelling tradition. As she says, "I
remember only a small part." She does, however, understand and convey
the importance of that part to the larger story. The reader understands
that Silko is not attempting to do ethnography as an anthropologist

might; rather, she is simply sharing what she remembers, and that sharing is the life of the story. The story's reality is in the telling, not in the rarefied air of language or history. The stories live lives of their own.

Silko retells a favorite story of Aunt Susie's, that of the little girl who wanted some *yashtoah* and ran away from home when she did not get it. In a running commentary set in italics, Silko explains yashtoah (the crust on cornmeal mush) and other elements of the story that may need elaboration for her contemporary, and probably nonnative, audience. Even this technique is part of the telling. When asked about the difference between writing and storytelling, Silko responded: "There's something pretty wonderful about oral narrative the way it was practiced at Laguna Pueblo because it's always contemporaneous—past, present, and future always in one moment. Because the storyteller footnotes herself and makes fun of herself and recollects."[3] In an interview with Dexter Fisher, she notes, "This is the beauty of the old way. You can stop the storyteller and ask questions and have things explained"(Fisher, 22).

Additions to the story are as much a part of the telling as the original version. This observation has broader implications than for the telling of a particular story. We recall that Betonie was able to perform the appropriate ceremony for Tayo because he changed the ritual, and although "the people mistrust this greatly," it is necessary for the survival of the people and the story or ritual. Silko comments:

> Every time a story is told, and this is one of the beauties of the oral tradition, each telling is a new and unique story, even if it's repeated word for word by the same teller sitting in the same chair. . . . Nobody saves stories. Writing down a story . . . doesn't save them in the sense of saving their life within a community. Stories stay alive within the community like the Laguna Pueblo community because the stories have a life of their own. . . . It's only the western Europeans who have this inflated pompous notion that every word, everything that's said or done is real important, and it's got to live on and on forever. (Barnes, 51–52)

This comment highlights one of Silko's themes, namely, change and how we recognize and deal with it.

The next character to appear from Silko's early life is Marie Anaya, Grandmother A'mooh. Silko's great-grandmother was from Paguate and married Robert G. Marmon after her sister, who had been married to him, died. She too was a graduate of Carlisle Indian School. Here we are told the story, often repeated by Silko in interviews, of Robert Marmon taking his two boys, Hank and Kenneth, into a hotel in Albuquerque, where the manager stopped him to tell him to use the restaurant's back entrance because he had Indians with him. Robert Marmon's reply was, "These are my sons," and he never set foot in the hotel again, "even years later / when they began to allow Indians inside." It is no accident, of course, that this story surfaces in Silko's interviews. It is a concrete manifestation of the symbolic registers seen in the first photograph and in the history of racism in America. It is no accident either that the first short story, "Storyteller," follows upon this account. "Storyteller" is a dark tale of racism and revenge but also of the integrity of stories and their tellers. The young woman in the story follows to the highest degree her mother's instruction about stories: "It will take a long time, but the story must be told. There must not be any lies" (26). In the end she refuses to tell the story the lawyer wants to provide, choosing instead the integrity of her own incriminating story. It is easy to see Silko herself in this story, refusing to tell lies about her family and serving the interests of the story rather than her self-interest.

After "Storyteller" the memories of Grandmother A'mooh are picked up once again. Silko called her A'mooh because that was the term of endearment she spoke to Leslie and her sisters while they stayed with her. It is possible to see a connection between the grandmother and granddaughter in "Storyteller" and Grandmother A'mooh and Silko. Of all the women in Silko's life, Marie Anaya seems to have had the most influence, possibly because she kept the Marmon girls while their mother worked. There is a photograph in the middle of the story about Grandmother A'mooh that shows her reading to Silko's sisters Wendy and Gigi. The grandmother is reading from a children's book, perhaps *Brownie the Bear,* which Silko recalls from her childhood, and she has a wonderful expression on her face that connotes both intense concentration and carefree enchantment. Wendy and Gigi are rapt, staring at the book as they press against either side of their grandmother. After completing Grandmother A'mooh's story, which ends with her going to stay with Aunt Bessie before she dies, Silko includes the journey poem "Indian Song: Survival," which speaks of mountainlion pursuing and catching a female narrator. Among other things, it is a poem about the inevitability of death.

One of the more enigmatic of Aunt Susie's stories concerns two girls searching for their mother during a devastating flood. They finally make their way to higher ground, specifically the top of a mesa, to find the rest of the village there but not their mother. As the people sit down to

wait out the flood, they all turn to stone, including the two little girls who never found their mother. The explanation Silko provides at the end of the story is important for understanding *Storyteller*. She writes: "The story ends there. / Some of the stories / Aunt Susie told / have this kind of ending. / There are no explanations" (42). There is a discomforting dynamic at work where stories must be told without any lies, and interpretation is open ended and sometimes inconclusive. It provides a healthy corrective to reductionistic approaches to interpretation fostered by anthropology, but it leaves readers, apparently including Silko herself, without explanations. This is an interesting fact in itself since it divorces stories from their interpretation or at least from the need to be unambiguous. At the same time it increases their enigmatic quality and elevates them above their "meaning." One way to understand this dichotomy between the integrity of the teller and the enigma of the story is to see the story as sacred and the teller's motivation as a ritual attitude. Just as a ritual creates sacred time and space that are ineffable, so does a story. The attitude of the participant in the ritual is crucial, not because it will destroy the ritual's integrity but because it will affect that of the participant. The ritual lives a life of its own, and stories have their own lives apart from their meaning to individuals.

Reducing *Storyteller* to sections does a disservice to the reader and the work. It collapses the fragile web spun by the tellers into categories that are abstract and remote from the stories themselves. I mention this because the next pages of *Storyteller* lend themselves to the sectional approach more easily than the others only because they deal thematically with the Yellow Woman motif. Most of the criticism of *Storyteller* takes this approach largely because it is a useful way to understand the diverse genres and forms in the book. What is lost in the translation from the reading experience of *Storyteller* to the categorization of the forms or sections there is tremendous. Although the next pages of the book concern the Yellow Woman motif, it is reductive to call it a Yellow Woman section and to go on and divide the book up like a pie. The more appropriate image to use, drawn from Silko herself, is that of the spiderweb, which offers a labyrinthine, associative approach rather than a linear, categorical approach.

As noted earlier, Yellow Woman may be the defining story for Silko's work. The Yellow Woman story appears in everything from *Ceremony*, where it helps us to understand Tayo's mother, to the poem "When Sun Came to Riverwoman," where it provides a backdrop for the images evoked. The importance of the Yellow Woman story to Silko's body of

work would be difficult to overestimate. Not surprisingly, Melody
Graulich edited a collection of essays just on "Yellow Woman." This volume appears in the Women Writers: Texts and Contexts series of Rutgers University Press and analyzes the story from a variety of perspectives. The next pages of *Storyteller* include the short story "Yellow
Woman" ; the poems "Cottonwood," "The Time We Climbed Snake
Mountain," and "Storytelling" ; several personal and historical stories;
several photographs; and a traditional Laguna tale that involves the
twins. In all of these "stories" Yellow Woman figures prominently
whether she is explicitly named or implied from her journey. Yellow
Woman is essentially a woman who leaves the demands of the everyday
world for the pleasures and mysteries of a world she has not encountered
before. The plot usually involves a woman going down to the river to
fetch water and encountering a mysterious man (or animal) who then
takes her to his home and keeps her for a time before she returns. In
some stories she returns pregnant with the twins of Laguna mythology,
but in others she simply returns with the water and not much is said.

Yellow Woman or Kochininako should not become a version of the
white, middle- or upper-class American woman who is simply looking
for something to displace the boredom in her life. Yellow Woman is not
a character from a romance novel; rather, she is a person willing to
explore and cross boundaries for the sake of relationships. According to
Silko, "What's operating in those stories of Kochininako is this attrac-
tion, this passion, this connection between the human world and the
animal and spirit worlds. Buffalo Man is a buffalo, and he can be in the
form of a buffalo, but there is this link, and the link is sealed with sexual
intimacy, which is emblematic of that joining of two worlds" (Barnes,
57). Yellow Woman, then, is not an escape story; rather, it is a story
about relation and the dangers and benefits of discovering a relationship
between yourself and the world.

After the Yellow Woman stories comes an interesting account of
Silko's own writing. Walking past her neighbor Nora's house, Silko
learns that Nora's grandchildren brought home a library book with her
coyote poem in it. Nora informs Silko that she enjoyed telling the children about coyote but remembers her grandfather taking longer to tell
it. Silko responds that "that's the trouble with writing . . . You can't go
on and on the way we do." This brief story offers an insight into Silko's
authorial consciousness, for she knows what is being lost in the transition from voice to page. At the same time, she recognizes that the stories transcend their medium and some translation is possible. She goes

on to fill in the details provided by Nora where Grandpa would begin telling the story only after being given an appropriate gift, such as roasted piñon nuts or a chunk of jerky. By highlighting the differences between writing and storytelling in a story, Silko subsumes the difference between the two, giving preference to the story over the medium.

The following stories engage various aspects of Laguna mythology or its relation to contemporary life. One extended tale dominates *Ceremony* and concerns the magician who comes to the village displaying Ck'o'yo magic and seducing the people, including the twins, away from the corn altar. Heroes are dispatched to correct the problem by making offerings to the corn mother and performing certain tasks for her. The phrases "You see, it wasn't easy" and "See, these things were complicated" appear in italics and signal that Silko's voice is emending the older story. These phrases echo the imperative in "Storyteller" that the story must be told without lies. The phrases also foreshadow the following piece, "Poem for Myself and Mei-Mei: Concerning Abortion," where things are not easy and the story is truthfully told. In conjunction with the situations described in various stories, phrases like these prevent readers from easily romanticizing Silko's work. These are hard words not easily assimilated into convenient mythologies of acculturation. These are stories of survival, and because survival is not easy and the story must be told as is, Silko is not shy about revealing all aspects of the tales.

Following these is the compelling "Tony's Story," which details the troubles of a recently returned Laguna veteran named Leon. Leon is harassed by a state highway patrolman for no reason other than the fact that he is a Native American. Leon's friend Tony has trouble understanding this until he determines that the patrolman is actually masquerading as a witch. When he interprets the situation in this way, Tony's only option is to treat the patrolman as a witch and burn him, which he does. As the body burns, storm clouds appear on the horizon, signaling the end to the long drought. Stories like this one reveal another important dimension of *Storyteller,* namely, the function of the ancient stories in a world drastically different from the one that generated them. Betonie in *Ceremony* is the typical representative of Silko's beliefs on this issue. The rituals and the stories live only if they change. To freeze them in time is to kill them just as surely as replacing them will destroy them. The stories must have continuity to perform their function, and that continuity is between the past and the present as well as between the creators and destroyers of the land. This belief is illustrated especially well in Silko's story, included in *Ceremony,* of the origin of white people. White people are the result of powerful witchery, and this beginning is lived out in the present with the penchant for destruction evidenced in the use of "rocks with veins of green and yellow and black" that will "lay the final pattern . . . and explode everything." That the story is set in italics throughout shows Silko's self-consciousness about her own story but also her realization that it belongs with the other stories. The fact that she places these ancient tales in juxtaposition to her own short stories and reminiscences relates them to each other and provides the necessary continuity for them to survive.

The two photographs that appear between Silko's story and the traditional story "Estoy-eh-muut and the Kunideeyahs" depict this phenomenon well. Both photographs are taken by Lee Marmon. The first shows an old woman, possibly Navajo, in traditional dress and jewelry; the other is a landscape shot of the desert with sharp peaks in the background. The note to the second photograph tells us that the Navajos believe that the peaks were formed by blood dropping from a monster slain by the twins. The two images almost converse as landscape and identity blend, and we imagine the woman as a mother and the peaks as a battleground. Juxtaposition, however, is not enough; the stories must be woven together like a web. The source of this web must be the mother herself, grandmother spider, who spins the stories out of her belly with love for her creation. All the lovers of creation then share in this magic. As Ku'oosh says in *Ceremony,* storytelling demands great patience and love. Patience and love provide the necessary continuity for the stories to live on, and at the heart of all of Silko's work is the representation of such patience and love.

The traditional stories in these pages include the influential story "Estoy-eh-muut and the Kunideeyahs," where Kochininako (Yellow Woman) is killed because she is a secret member of the Kunideeyahs (the destroyers). Silko attempted to retell this story on film in 1980. Estoy-eh-muut kills Yellow Woman by rolling at her a coiled ring of yucca fiber that becomes a rattlesnake. There are many versions of this story.[4] *Storyteller* also contains the account, found in *Ceremony,* of Corn Woman's jealousy of her sister, Reed Woman, who was always taking a bath, which prompts Reed Woman to go to the original place down below, taking the rain with her. Preceding this story is a brief song called "The Go-Wa-Peu-Zi Song," which in English comes across as "Of the clouds / and rain clouds / and growth of corn / I sing." The connections between this ancient chant and the story of the two sisters are obvious. After a story about Silko's father and his interest in photography and clouds, Silko includes another Ck'o'yo magician story, only this one is named Kaup'a'ta, or the Gambler. This wonderful story describes Sun Man's successful journey to free the rain clouds that the Gambler is holding after winning them in a bet. With the help of Spider-Woman, Sun Man outwits the Gambler, beating him at his own game and returning the clouds to the sky and life to the land. The story ends with Sun Man opening the doors of the rooms that hold the rain clouds and saying to them "I have found you! / Come on out. Come home again. / Your Mother, the Earth is crying for you. / Come home, children, come home" (169). Silko continues to focus upon the land by including an excerpt of a letter to Lawson F. Inada, in which she discusses plants that have appeared for the first time after a long period of rain. She recalls stories of water in abundance in places that are now so dry that they seem different landscapes altogether.

With the letter to Inada, Silko begins to shift the scene of storytelling to the present day. Following the letter is her rendition of a story told to her by her friend and fellow poet Simon Ortiz from Acoma. Entitled "Uncle Tony's Goat," this story evokes the feeling of appreciation one has at the first experience of forgiveness. Following that story is the poem "How to Write a Poem about the Sky," which is dedicated to the students of Bethel Middle School in Bethel, Alaska. Continuing with her own work, Silko follows with three more poems, "In Cold Storm Light," "Prayer to the Pacific," and "Horses at Valley Store," all with sacramental qualities that celebrate and magnify the land and its creatures. Finally, she offers a brief but wonderful story about the birth of her father just as the Angelus bells were ringing in the church. The bells appear in the following short story, "The Man to Send Rain Clouds," which is about the death of a local man and the conflict of traditions that surrounds his burial, his Laguna friends arranging for a traditional burial while the local priest unwittingly participates in it by dropping holy water onto the body, which ends up producing rain clouds.

A photograph of Grandpa Hank reading is placed near a brief story about one of his Navajo friends who brought him gifts. Grandpa Hank would go around his store gathering up items to give his friend in return. This tradition comes from a story wherein some Navajos stole a number of sheep from Laguna but were tracked down and caught. When they were asked why they did it, they replied that they were starving. The Lagunas told them that they had only to ask and food would be given them. Laguna Feast Day evolved from that day, in which no Navajo may be refused anything from any Laguna home. The old

friend of Grandpa Hank was following this tradition. Silko recounts seeing fewer and fewer Navajos come to the feast and, with her father,
watching the last wagon come and go. She also includes a photograph of
Laguna Fiesta from the 1950s that shows covered wagons mingling
with automobiles and pickup trucks.

The next pages contain stories that cluster around the hunting
theme, which intertwines with memories of Grandpa Hank since it was
he who taught Leslie to hunt. Following the poem "Deer Dance: For
Your Return" is a short account that explains the nature of hunting,
especially deer, in Laguna society. In the fall Laguna hunters go to the
hills to hunt deer, and the deer willingly give themselves to the hunters
so that the people will not starve. Late in the winter a Deer Dance is
held to honor the deer who gave themselves that year. Once the dance is
done, the deer will return in spirit form to the mountains to be reborn in
new bodies that will some day be sacrificed again.[5] The mythology of
this ritual permeates Silko's work, providing the backdrop for much of
her poetry and implied in much of her fiction. In fact, one could argue
that it is precisely this ritual attitude that Tayo must adopt in order to
become whole again, namely, the recognition that the earth and her
creatures, when respected, give willingly of life and sustenance. Again,
the attitude of the person involved is what is important and determines
the outcome of the ritual or the story. Silko writes, "Only when [the
Deer Dance] has been properly done will the spirits be able to return to
the mountain and be reborn into more deer who will, remembering the
reverence and appreciation of the people, once more come home with
the hunters" (191).

After a story about her Grandfather Hank that includes a photograph of him standing by his 1933 Auburn motorcar, Silko offers a
poem titled "A Hunting Story," dedicated to H. C. Marmon. Following
the poem is another reminiscence about Grandpa Hank, which tells of
his driving a wagon and a buggy around Laguna and Paguate. Apparently, he drove tourists around most of the time, but once in 1908 he
drove several people from the Smithsonian to Katsi'ma, or Enchanted
Mesa. He recalls their putting everything they found on top into boxes
that they shipped back to Washington, D.C. The story ends with
Grandpa Hank surmising, "You know / probably all those boxes of
things / they took from Enchanted Mesa / are still just sitting somewhere / in the basement of some museum" (198–99).

The hunting stories continue with the poems "Preparations," "Story
from Bear Country," and the older story of the boy who turned into a

bear. This unnamed tale is a fine example of Silko's interest in the relationship between humans and animals, articulating as it does the dangers involved in intercourse between different outlooks. Changing into a bear is a strong metaphor for change itself, and although Silko clearly values the relationship between human beings and all things, she also recognizes a dual danger. One danger documented in *Ceremony* is overdetermining one element in the creation as the destroyers do; they value themselves above all things instead of valuing their relationship with all things. The other danger is found in the story of the boy who turned into a bear. Silko, speaking of his loved ones who come to rescue him, puts it this way: "They couldn't just grab the child. / They couldn't simply take him back / because he would be in-between forever / and probably he would die" (209). To be "in-between forever" is not to be related at all to either humans or animals. In fact "in-between" is probably as good a description of Tayo's problem as any. By virtue of being in-between, Tayo and, by implication, humans in general risk being disconnected from the world that holds us in its web.

With the hunting stories associated with Grandpa Hank, *Storyteller* picks up speed in the reader's time frame. Anecdotes appear more frequently and are shorter than the other recorded memories, poems appear more frequently, and there is more white space on the page. The reading moves faster, and there is a slight tilt toward the present rather than the past. Whether this change in rhythm is intended is hard to say, but the cadence is clearly different. One reason for this change may be the fact that the present moves faster than the past, and stories from the present are more immediate and easier to assimilate. When Silko is telling an ancient tale, a silent reverence envelops the story as if something old and holy were being unearthed. Present-day stories, by virtue of their immediacy in time and familiarity in reference, are more easily assimilated into the reading experience. This observation may well reflect a Western bias on my part, one that derives from a particular notion of time that is more apt to value something as sacred when it is old rather than new because the older is closer to the beginning, the original. Such prejudices are not necessarily endemic to Native American culture, but they are likely to appear in the minds of nonnative readers.

The last pages of the book highlight the coyote theme. Two short stories, "A Geronimo Story" and "Coyote Holds a Full House in His Hand" are about trickery and humor, as are some personal stories about roosters that are told in a letter to James Wright and in a recollection of

Grandma Lillie. "Toesh: A Laguna Coyote Story" is here as is the older Laguna legend that inspired Silko's poem. There are contemporary accounts of Fiesta, where a group of Navajos found a good stash for their alcohol until the tribal police found it; the tribal police do not fare well in the story because they are the reason few Navajos now come to the feast. The poem "Skeleton Fixer" appears here as "a piece of a bigger story they tell around Laguna and Acoma too," followed by a poignant reminiscence of Grandpa Hank's telling the story of Apaches who killed his grand-uncles. The poem "Storyteller's Escape" is placed near the end of the book and describes how a story saves an old storyteller's life by creating a reality in which she was safe from her enemies. The story-teller's lines at the beginning of the poem summarize her experience: "With these stories of ours / we can escape almost anything / with these stories we will survive" (247).

It is easy to see autobiographical content in this poem, especially given its placement near the end of the book. Such an interpretation is justified, provided we do not understand it as a kind of postmodern irony where Silko is being disingenuous. She is not trying to escape the responsibility of the stories; on the contrary, she is celebrating the power of the story to provide for the creation of a reality of its own. The story is the escape, but it is not an escape from reality; rather, it is a flight to the reality of the story. The difference between the two is important, which is why at the beginning Silko has the storyteller speaking of survival and remembering the dear ones. These are not language games but living realities generated by the story. That this is her best story is not surpris-ing; it is a tale about the power of stories. That it appears with coyote stories is no accident, for this is an account of trickery and tricksters who above all survive.

The book ends appropriately enough with three photographs and two coyote stories. One of the photographs shows Silko in the Tucson mountains near her home in Arizona. The other two are from earlier times and show Grandpa Hank in Abie Abraham's store and four men and two boys, including her great-grandpa Robert G. Marmon and her father as a boy. The juxtaposition of these photographs, which are sepa-rated only by the notes to all the photographs, provides a moment for reflection on the book as a whole and asks readers to draw the lines con-necting Leslie Marmon Silko, her grandfather Hank, and Robert G. Marmon and his kin in the last photograph. Of course, the lines have been drawn already in the previous pages of the book, and the reader recognizes the pattern that has been in place all along. The people are connected by stories and land, the two entities celebrated throughout the book.

The coyote stories that end the book reflect both sides of coyote, the tragic and the comic. The first story is Silko's own account of the anthropologists who put Laguna on the academic map, Franz Boas and Elsie Clews Parsons. She recounts how Boas had to leave the construction of Laguna grammar to Parsons because Keresan is a tonal language and Boas was tone deaf. She recalls that her great-grandpa Marmon told one of the coyote stories to Parsons. It was about Coyote trying to carry water in her mouth back to her pups, but meadowlark teases her each time, causing her to lose the water until the pups die of thirst. This story represents the tragic side of Coyote's misfortunes largely because she is tricked not by herself but by someone else. Silko's interpretation of this event evokes a spirit of tragedy as well. She reports that ethnologists blame the Marmon brothers for much trouble at Laguna and "I am sure much of it is true."[6] All Silko knows of her great-grandfather, she writes, is "the stories my family told / and the old photographs." These photographs help Silko to comprehend "that he had come to understand this world / differently." She believes that he told that particular coyote story to Parsons to reflect a belief: "No matter what is said to you by anyone / you must take care of those most dear to you" (256).

The book ends with the comic trickster story "Coyote Holds a Full House in His Hand," a risqué story about a man who devises an ingenious "cure" for dizziness that has women lining up to have their thighs rubbed with juniper ashes by this contemporary coyote. His success is credited to the fact that "he was so good at making up stories to justify why things happened the way they did." Ending the book with this coyote story leaves the reader smiling as the last strand of the web is spun. The story leads us to believe that even the poorest of us, like the man in the story, can be elevated by the power of a good story.

Bernard Hirsch has stated quite correctly that "the interrelationships between the various narrative episodes and photographs throughout is so rich and intricate that any attempt to formally divide the work into sections or categories would be arbitrary at best, of necessity reductive, and at worst misleading."[7] I would add that even an attempt to trace these interrelationships in a model of the reader's experience in time, as I try to do in the previous pages, falls short of detailing completely the craft involved in the writing and telling. One of the finest articles on *Storyteller*, Hirsch's essay explains the dynamic of reading at work in this way: "In *Storyteller*, the reader learns by accretion. Successive narrative episodes cast long shadows both forward and back, lending different or complementary shades of meaning to those preceding them and offering perspectives from which to consider those that follow. Such perspectives are then themselves often expanded or in some way altered as the new material reflects back upon them" (Hirsch, 3). This description of the reading process of *Storyteller* is profound and helpful and aptly describes the reader's experience with this book. *Storyteller* can also be read as an anthology of Silko's work, especially the short stories.

Short Stories

The short story seems to be the form most suited to Silko's talents. We recall that this was the genre she used for her first stories and that she was first known as a short-story writer. Almost all of her short stories are found in *Storyteller*. In an interview with Donna Perry, she describes her relation to the various forms of writing: "I'm a sort of structure nut, and sometimes I think the failings of my short stories are that they are too tightly structured—even though I don't do it consciously. They end up clicking too much together like poems or something" (Perry, 333). Most readers will know Silko either through her much anthologized short stories or through *Ceremony*, which began as a short story.

"Storyteller"

Silko's signature story may well be "Storyteller" because it deals dramatically and in a highly condensed form with almost all the issues addressed in her other work. The connection between stories and land figures prominently as does the ability of a story to engage both life and death in the telling. There is trickery and tragedy in these pages as well. In "Storyteller" a young woman who lives with her grandmother and an old man learns of the true cause of the death of her parents. The story begins with the woman in jail, contemplating the merging of horizons she sees out of her small window. We learn the reason she is there through a series of flashbacks, separated by added white space, that recount her activities up to the present. Her story is one not uncommon for Native American children from Silko's generation; she is sent away to boarding school as a child and punished when she does not speak English. Returning for the summer she learns that her grandmother has died, her joints "swollen with anger." For her new home she must choose between the local priest, who will send her away to another school, or the old man, who is not her grandfather and wants her to stay so that he can molest her. She chooses what is for her the lesser of two evils and stays with the old man.

The woman, who remains nameless, begins to explore the artificial boundaries drawn by the Gussucks (whites) and the old man. She sleeps with a red-haired Gussuck who tapes a photograph of a woman being mounted by a big dog on the wall as they have sex. Meanwhile, the old man is beginning a story about the end of things in the village. "It is approaching," he says. "As it comes, ice will push across the sky." The story concerns a giant polar bear stalking a hunter on the Bering Sea ice, and it unfolds slowly and in great detail. As primary storyteller, the old man caresses the story, "repeating the words again and again like gentle strokes." The young woman also becomes a storyteller in the end as she lives out her own hunt. She enacts revenge upon the storeman by leading him onto the river ice that she knows in great detail but he knows not at all. As she carefully picks her way, he rushes headlong at her and falls into the deadly cold of the river. Her lawyer wants her to tell the story that will exonerate her, that she was being pursued by a man who intended to kill her and that his death was accidental. She refuses because of her grandmother's statement that the story "must be told" and "there must not be any lies."

Written during Silko's time in Alaska, "Storyteller" is her attempt to engage the oral tradition with a different landscape. The American Southwest is an area of contrasts from colors to climates, but the Alaskan landscape of "Storyteller" is one of glaring uniformity. In fact, the dominant image of the story is the merging of land and sky to the point where they are indistinguishable. The woman who becomes the storyteller "told herself it wasn't a good sign for the sky to be indistinguishable from the river ice, frozen solid and white against the earth." A similar idea is expressed in the poem "How to Write a Poem about the Sky," included in *Storyteller*. The lines "You see the sky now / but the earth / is lost in it / and there are no horizons / It is all / a single breath" echo the dramatic change in landscape that Silko herself experienced. That the elimination of difference in the landscape should be a dangerous thing, as stated in "Storyteller," indicates that the elimination of difference in other areas may be dangerous as well. As the story plays out, this observation turns out to be quite true. The inability of the woman's parents to tell the difference between liquor and alcohol or poison, the inability of the storeman to tell the difference between solid ice and thin ice, and the unwillingness of the old man to tell the difference between the story and his life in the cabin all signal danger to the people involved.

Color plays an important role in the story for the same reason, whether it is the forbidding whiteness of sky and earth or the predominance of yellow in the Gussucks' material culture (the insulation of the Gussuck buildings, the covering of their large machines that sink into the bog as they roll off the barge, and the yellow dog with matted hair that sleeps in the store). In this story, yellow takes on a different connotation because of the altered landscape. This is the yellow of the early part of *Ceremony,* of Tayo's urine and vomit, not the yellow of corn, pollen, sandstone, and Yellow Woman.

"Telling the difference" seems to be what is at stake in the story. The woman knows the difference between a story that will exonerate her and one that reflects her plans, but she refuses to tell that story because it is not true. Instead she says, "I killed him, but I don't lie." The real danger is the obliteration of difference itself symbolized by the merging of horizons and the coming ice that, according to the old man, will "push across the sky." The obliteration of contrast is the obliteration of boundaries, and boundaries are what form identity. The encroachment of the bland uniformity of white culture, like the approaching ice that will turn everything white, portends the loss of identity through the loss of difference. This radical fear of uniformity causes the young woman to nail the red tin of old fuel cans to the walls of the log house, not because it will help with the insulation but because it offers a boundary, a border, a demarcation of difference: "She felt a chill when she saw how the sky and land were already losing their boundaries, already becoming lost in each other. But the red tin penetrated the thick white color of earth and sky; it defined the boundaries like a wound revealing the ribs and heart of caribou about to bolt and be lost to the hunter forever" (28).

The story ends as the old man finally confronts the bear that is about to devour him and the young woman tells her story of killing the storeman over and over. The story must be told without any lies, and in the end there are none. Even the old man's story is true since he lives it out to the literal end. Stories are not simply entertainment or fantasy but invoke the realities that they describe. Stories are generative, and they may generate death as well as survival.

"Lullaby"

"Lullaby" is one of the most anthologized of Silko's short stories and appears, among other places, in Martha Foley's *Best American Short Stories of 1975.* It is the story of a man and a woman, Navajos named Chato and Ayah, who are the parents of three children. The older son, Jimmie, has been killed in the war, and all they have left of him is an old army blanket he sent them. This blanket becomes central to the story because it is the only protection they have against the snow. Ayah has two other children, and she thinks about them reaching for tufts of wool just as she is reaching for tufts of snow. Ayah is "an old woman now, and her life had become memories," and the story proceeds, much like "Story-teller," by recounting those memories. As she watches the snow fill in her tracks, we recognize that the story is having the opposite effect, namely, of uncovering Ayah's tracks.

As she recalls the birth of her firstborn, Jimmie, Ayah's thoughts jump from naming him for the summer morning to hearing of his death. The juxtaposition of these images is striking and alerts the reader to the fact that this is not a lullaby story about the innocence of children. On the contrary, this is a story about the horrors of adulthood, but it also reflects the ability to weave all of the events of one's life into a story. Jimmie's death is not the only horror Ayah has faced. Chato is fired from his job as a ranch hand when a horse throws him and breaks his leg, and she knows that if Jimmie were alive, he could have worked for his father. Her younger children, Danny and Ella, are taken to foster homes after she is forced to sign release forms that she does not understand. Jimmie would have understood the writing and told her not to sign. We learn that the children had tuberculosis and were taken to a sanitarium in Colorado and that she hated Chato for teaching her to sign her name. When the rancher repays Chato's years of loyalty by throwing them out of their gray boxcar shack, Ayah and Chato move back to the hogan in which Ayah was born and where they keep a few sheep. As the story moves back into the present, Ayah must return to the bar where Chato had stayed to cash their government check. She looks for him in the bar, ignoring the looks of the Spaniards who see her as "a spider crawling slowly across the room." Finally, she finds Chato shuffling down the sidewalk. She accompanies him to some boulders to block the wind as the snow continues to fall. As the clouds clear and the "icy stillness" descends from the night sky, Ayah bundles Chato up in Jimmie's blanket and sings him a lullaby as he dies.

Images of weaving dominate this story from the army blanket that appears throughout to the new wool that Ayah compares with the snow, to the sheep that they end up keeping after being thrown off the ranch. As with much of Silko's work, these images lead us to think metaphorically of similar but different things. Language, especially as it appears in the chant at the end, is woven around the dying Chato just as the army blanket is. Memory, too, serves as a blanket that warms Ayah and allows her to continue living despite the horrible conditions she faces. The story itself weaves readers into the narrative where they are wrapped in the memories of Ayah's life and current circumstances. Such weaving, the story suggests, is all we have. Ayah recalls that the blankets her mother made were woven so tight that rain rolled off them like bird feathers and that they kept her warm on cold nights on the hogan floor. The struggle recounted here is as old as humanity: It is the struggle to survive. Blankets and other human creations are attempts to strengthen our bodies against the onslaughts of climate. Words and memories are human creations that brace us against the onslaughts of pain and loss. They wrap around us like blankets but never quite cover us completely. We must all yield to the earth and sky in the end, and it is this comfort that the lullaby provides: "The earth is your mother / she holds you. / The sky is your father, / he protects you. / Sleep, / sleep. / Rainbow is your sister, / she loves you. / The winds are your brothers, / they sing to you. / Sleep, / sleep. / We are together always / We are together always / There was never a time / when this / was not so" (51). This lullaby is the only comfort provided, but it is enough for Ayah because it is a blanket of words that enfolds them both.

"Yellow Woman"

"Yellow Woman" is Silko's retelling of the ancient and provocative Pueblo legend of Kochininako. Franz Boas, the anthropologist who with his protégé, Elsie Clews Parsons, provides much of the ethnographic data on the Pueblos, sees some common elements among these ancient stories. They almost always concern an abduction and/or seduction of a woman who happens to be at the river drawing water. The woman usually offers a reason that she cannot go with the man, and that reason usually has to do with chores or other concerns of the home. The man then, by means of threats or other persuasion, compels the woman to accompany him to his mountain home. As in many journey myths, the woman who is entering the new world is given tasks to perform to save her life. Winning her place there, she then experiences a passionate affair with the man and in some cases becomes pregnant with the heroic twins of Pueblo mythology. The man often takes the form of Sun Man, Whirlwind Man, Cliff Dweller, or Buffalo Man (Boas, 218 – 62). The Buffalo Man version is included in *Storyteller* in poetic form as "Cottonwood Part Two: Buffalo Story."

As discussed earlier, the Yellow Woman stories may provide the generative motifs for much of Silko's work by virtue of including the ideas of relation, boundary, and identity as well as time, story, and survival. The story stands out from its very first line, "My thigh clung with his dampness." From that opening the reader follows Yellow Woman on a journey of tremendous danger, passion, and meaning. Beginning with the story already underway makes Silko's version of the Yellow Woman tale move more quickly and dramatically. The old paradoxes and mysteries are there, however, and she even makes the story more enigmatic in places. Like most of her other stories and poems, "Yellow Woman" finds its genesis in personal and communal memory. Silko recalls hearing many Yellow Woman stories in her childhood, and those generated their own reality when she would walk by the river.

> The river was a place to meet boyfriends and lovers and so forth. I used to wander around down there and try to imagine walking around the bend and just happening to stumble upon some beautiful man. Later on I realized that these kinds of things that I was doing when I was fifteen are exactly the kinds of things out of which stories like the Yellow Woman story [originates]. I finally put the two together: the adolescent longings and the old stories, that plus the stories around Laguna at the time about people who did, in fact, just in recent times use the river as a meeting place. (Evers and Carr, 29).

The moment when Silko finally "put the two together"—the adolescent longings and the old stories—is definitive. It provided her with the connection between land, identity, and story that her characters explore in various ways. That Yellow Woman should be the story that crystallizes these ideas for her is not unexpected. Paula Gunn Allen notes that "Kochinnenako,[8] Yellow Woman, is in some sense a name that means Woman-Woman because among the Keres, yellow is the color for women. . . . In many ways Kochinnenako is a role model. . . . She is, one might say, the Spirit of Woman" (Allen, 88). "Yellow Woman," then, is at the very least a foundational text in Silko's body of work and offers a representation of her most meaningful ideas in a few pages of prose.

Silko's short story highlights the issues of boundary and identity. Much of the dialogue centers on the identity of the woman, who is not quite sure she is in fact Yellow Woman. Much of the action concerns the crossing and recrossing of borders or boundaries. These different spaces, the river, the mountain, the pueblo, the man's body, all offer Yellow Woman an opportunity to define herself. She tries to leave when they are still down by the river but reaches out and touches the man's body in order to tell him this and ends up going with him. Later, up on the mountain, she leaves for the pueblo, but the next scene has her at his side. Who she is, is determined in good measure by where she is. Silva, whose name in Spanish means *collection* or *anthology,* takes her up on the mountain and shows her the borders of Navajo, Pueblo, and Texan lands (Ruoff, 12). He has no doubt as to her identity, calling her "Yellow Woman" or "little Yellow Woman" throughout the story. Instead of having her perform some superhuman task to save her life, Silva asks only that she fry some potatoes, although he does tell her that she will do what he wants. Her fear of him is countered and overcome by (or perhaps wrapped up in) her desire for him, and that desire causes her to follow him when he takes a rustled beef carcass to market. Met on the trail by the white rancher who has been the victim of Silva's rustling, Silva and Yellow Woman part. She goes back up the trail while he stays to confront the unarmed rancher. After hearing four shots, Yellow Woman cannot seem to find Silva's home and turns her horse down the hill toward the pueblo. Just as she could not see the pueblo from the river, now she cannot find Silva's home. This inability to see signals a change in her identity as she crosses back into her everyday world. Her return home, as in the traditional Yellow Woman stories, is unplanned (Ruoff, 14). She decides to make up a story about being kidnapped by a Navajo (which is not entirely untrue) because no one at her house could understand the type of journey she has returned from. Only her grandfather appreciated the old stories that provide a context for what has happened to her. By crossing and recrossing boundaries, she has experienced the sacred in a way that demonstrates the ultimate interrelationship of all things, including the stories to the land and identity.

"Tony's Story"

Silko's sophomore year in college was eventful. She became pregnant with her first son and married Dick Chapman. While pregnant, she began looking for classes that would not be too draining, and Dick suggested a creative writing class that would be an easy A. She recalls that she was thinking only of preparing for law school, but Dick's wisdom prevailed, and she took the creative writing class (Perry, 321–22). Three short stories came out of that first class, "Bravura," "Tony's Story," and "The Man to Send Rain Clouds." Although "The Man to Send Rain Clouds" was the first story to be published in a national magazine, "Tony's Story" was the first to appear in print.[9]

On Friday, April 11, 1952, a New Mexico state trooper named Nash García was shot with a .30-.30 and subsequently burned in his patrol car. Two brothers, Willie and Gabriel Felipe, were arrested and later sentenced to life imprisonment. Leslie Marmon was four years old when this event occurred, but the story floated around the Laguna community for some time and resurfaced in Silko's memory when she was asked to write a story in the creative writing class. Lawrence Evers reports that in a visit to Laguna-Acoma High School around 1976, "Silko found that well over half the children she read to were aware of [the image of García as an Indian-hater].¹⁰ It is not unusual that Silko would choose a historical event to base a story upon; she does the same thing with "The Man to Send Rain Clouds" and elements of other works. She weaves into the story many elements of the case, such as the veteran just home from service, the illegal wine, the type of gun, and the burning of the body. The most important element, however, is the belief in witchcraft. Long associated with the Rio Grande Pueblos and southwestern tribes in general, witchcraft has its own dynamics that are different from Western understanding.¹¹ This dimension of "Tony's Story" colors the entire piece. Like Willie Felipe and his brother, Tony believes that the policeman who is harassing Leon is a witch.

At issue in "Tony's Story" is truth, the truth of two different stories. We are presented with two ways of seeing the world, each of which is deemed unacceptable by the other. In one worldview the story is about a person in authority who violates the rules he is sworn to uphold by unfairly harassing an innocent person. The other story, and the one that prevails in the end, is that a witch has been loosed upon Tony and Leon and is dispatched in the only way that witches can be killed—by burning. The story begins, as many of Silko's do, with an assault by the climate. It is summer, and there has been no rain. After Tony kills the state police officer, he tells Leon that "everything is O.K. now," and the last line of the story reads "in the west, rain clouds were gathering." This ending, along with Tony's first-person narration, shifts the allegiance of the reader toward Tony's account.

There are other subtexts at work also, such as the one concerning identity. Tony, who has not been off the reservation, still believes and practices traditionally. Leon, on the other hand, has been in the army, and like Tayo he has seen that differences between Native Americans and whites can be dissolved by creating a greater difference between "Americans" and other groups. Back on the reservation, Leon expects this architecture of difference to be maintained. The state policeman, however, operates according to the old distinctions where "Indians" are the opposite of "Americans." Tony has trouble understanding Leon's new outlook. Seeing him at the feast, Tony reminds him that he will remember how to do the Corn Dance because he "was once more a part of the pueblo." After the first encounter where the big officer punches Leon for no reason and Leon promises revenge, Tony wonders "why men who came back from the army were troublemakers on the reservation." Leon must also deal with the clash of notions of difference. He learned about rights not on the reservation but in the army. He tells Tony that "We are just as good as them" and "We've got a right to be on this highway." Tony's perspective is that "Leon didn't seem to understand; he couldn't remember the stories that old Teofilo told." When Tony offers Leon the protection of an arrowhead to wear around his neck, Leon is incredulous that Tony would believe in that sort of thing and grabs instead the .30-.30 leaning against the wall, thereby demonstrating that his protection is now guns, not amulets.

"Tony's Story" is a provocative account of contrasting ways of seeing the world. Those differences are not theoretical but intensely personal and practical, so much so in fact that the title character is compelled to act in his friend's best interest by committing what is in one worldview a felony but in another a ritual act of heroism. The rain clouds do come at the end, indicating that Tony's story offers an explanation for what in any other story is mere coincidence.

"Uncle Tony's Goat"

This story is about a different Tony; in fact, it may not even qualify as a short story at all in traditional literary terms. Silko prefaces the story with a paragraph that describes its origin. Simon Ortiz, Silko's friend and fellow writer from Acoma, called her early one morning, and they had a good talk about goats. Afterward, Silko decided to write up a story that Ortiz told her on the phone. This is probably Ortiz's story as well, although proprietary rights to stories are not an issue at Laguna and Acoma. I include it among Silko's short stories because it is her rendition and has the same form (title in all capitals, two justified columns) that the other stories in *Storyteller* do. This is a wonderful tale about a boy (no doubt Ortiz) who shot arrows at his uncle's nanny goats and kids while the old, ornery billy goat looked on and took the boy into his memory. The billy goat was Uncle Tony's favorite because he had paid a lot for him and brought him from Quemado. No one but Uncle Tony could get near the goat, but one day Uncle Tony asked the boy to get the billy goat out of his pen. The stubborn goat did not move, and the boy complained to his uncle that he could not get him out, but Uncle Tony sent him back to try again. Then the goat charged the boy and sent him reeling. The boy felt guilty because his uncle had said that animals will not bother us unless we bother them. When he returned from school, the boy learned that the goat had run away after jumping out of the pen. After pursuing him for three days, Uncle Tony returned without him and said: "There wasn't ever a goat like that one, but if that's the way he's going to act, O.K. then. That damn goat got pissed off too easy anyway" (176). Uncle Tony smiled at his nephew as he said this, and "his voice was strong and happy."

We are led to believe that one of the other reasons that Uncle Tony and his goat got along so well was that they were so much alike: ornery and easily angered. The implication of his pronouncement at the end is that Uncle Tony values his nephew more than his beloved goat. There is also the sense that Uncle Tony realizes that he may appear to the boy as threatening and dangerous, which makes his gesture of kindness at the end all the more significant.

"The Man to Send Rain Clouds"

Here is one of Silko's early successes, a short story of only three pages that captures the meaning of stories, survival, and the continuation of the ancient rituals. "The Man to Send Rain Clouds" is also based on the goings-on at Laguna and was written from a newspaper account and the subsequent gossip about it. The story centers on old Teofilo, who has died at a sheep camp. Leon and his brother-in-law Ken drive up to check on him and find him under a big cottonwood tree. Leon ties a small feather in the old man's hair. We know from Silko's emendations to Aunt Susie's *yastoah* story that this is the traditional practice at Laguna. They also paint Teofilo's face and offer cornmeal and pollen to the wind. With these ritual acts they say, "Send us rain clouds, Grandfather." Driving back to the pueblo they encounter Father Paul, who asks if they found Teofilo. Leon tells the father that they were just out there and everything is okay now. He does not bother to tell the Father that Teofilo is also dead. When Father Paul tells them that Teofilo should not stay at the sheep camp alone, they respond that he will not be doing that anymore. Before he drives off, the priest encourages them to bring Teofilo to Mass. The ritual continues with the village bringing food by for the gravediggers and embracing Teofilo's family. After the funeral

Leon's wife suggests that if the priest sprinkled holy water over Grandpa, he might not be so thirsty. Thinking this is a fine idea, Leon goes down to the church to ask the priest to bring his holy water to the graveside. The priest is angry that he was not allowed to perform the last rites and thereby provide a Christian burial and decides that he cannot sprinkle the water without having performed the last rites and a funeral Mass. Leon accepts this argument and starts to leave, but the priest changes his mind after seeing Leon's response. At the graveside the priest wonders if there is a trick involved, if Teofilo is indeed dead. He suspects a ritual is being performed for a good harvest, since it is now March. Indeed, he is reminded of something as he watches the water disappear almost before it touches the sand, but his training prevents him from seeing this act as Leon and his family do, namely, as an offering for rain and by implication a good harvest. Leon is very satisfied and feels sure that the old man will provide the rain clouds now that he has been given water.

The story highlights an element of Silko's work that is often overlooked—her excellent gift of humor. She exhibits a native sense of humor in fine fashion in the dialogue with the priest.[12] Readers are in the know, and the priest is not, which accounts in part for the effect of Leon's careful omissions. Woven into the humor is a very serious tone of survival. Such ironies were the very means by which Native Americans were able to continue their traditional ceremonies under the scrutiny of white missionaries. By moving their spring ceremonies to Easter or their winter solstice ceremonies to Christmas and by adapting the rituals enough to pass as both, they were able to continue the traditions in some form. No doubt Betonie would approve.

"A Geronimo Story"

It is true that Laguna men were recruited by the U.S. Cavalry to help track the notorious Geronimo. These men, called the Laguna Regulars, appear in a photograph at the end of "A Geronimo Story." Once again, Silko uses history in the service of story. The story itself is told in first-person by Siteye, the nephew of one of these men. Andy is the boy who gets to go along with his Uncle because Siteye has a broken foot and needs help saddling his horse, although we suspect that there may be more involved in this wish, such as the desire to have the boy participate in a good story involving trickery and interpretation. Indeed, this is precisely what happens. The real hunt is for deer and perhaps to avoid being hunted by Geronimo. Andy narrates the hunt from a perspective that is years after the events, and we learn with the boy and Siteye about the power of language, a power that is greater than the military power of the U.S. Cavalry. The excursion is led by Captain Pratt, who heads the troops to Pie Town, although both he and Siteye know that Geronimo is not there. Captain Pratt and Siteye have a relationship of mutual respect, despite the fact that Pratt represents the colonial forces that have devastated Siteye's people, land, and culture. In fact, we are led to see Pratt as a version of Robert Marmon: They are both called "Squaw Man," they both marry Laguna women, and they both adopt Laguna ways. Pratt is a cipher for Silko's ambivalence, about her white ancestor. Contrasted with Pratt is the representative of white racism and ignorance, Major Littlecock. The humor of his name is blended with a deep disrespect in the evening discussions among the Laguna Regulars. The humor continues in the face of blatant racism when the unit arrives at Pie Town. There the white inhabitants display their distrust of the Lagunas, and Major Littlecock is in his element. Siteye's comment on it all is that it is too bad Geronimo is not there because he can think of no better place to wipe out. He goes on to suggest that if they see Geronimo and his warriors, they should send them to Pie Town. Andy contextualizes the situation from his position in the future:" 'Anybody can act violently—there's nothing to it; but not every person is able to destroy his enemy with words.' That's what Siteye always told me, and I respect him" (222). Andy continues to learn about trickery and language through the stories his uncle tells and the absence of the ultimate trickster, Geronimo. The final words of the story reflect the humor and literal misdirection that Andy has learned to appreciate when Siteye remarks, "You know that was a long way to go for deer hunting" (223). The humor of the story combines with the subversive intention of the storyteller to produce a profoundly political text that also delights. Not unexpectedly, this story appears near the end of the book (if we can call it an end). Silko has woven a coyote tale that also creates the storytellers' escape as it captures the reader.

"Coyote Holds a Full House in His Hand"

Like "A Geronimo Story," this final coyote story involves trickery and humor. Coyote in this case is a Laguna man who finds a way to outdo his Hopi counterparts in winning the sexual favors of the women in the village. Sonny Boy is a character right out of the coyote stories: lazy, unscrupulous, and eager to find pleasure that is unattached to work. His unwillingness to marry has cost him a girlfriend who is easily won by a Hopi man who is willing to work. He has instead set his sights on a widow by the name of Mrs. Sekakaku, whose chief attributes for Sonny Boy are "the creases and folds . . . and little rolls" of her body. His hopes for a sexual encounter are dashed when he arrives at her house to find her niece engaging her in earnest conversation about her Aunt Mamie's dizzy spells. Drawing on his ability to "make up stories to justify why things happened the way they did," he offers his services as a Laguna medicine man and suddenly becomes the center of attention. He instructs the women to gather all the women of Aunt Mamie's clan, and when they arrive, he lines them up in front of him. The "ceremony" consists of Sonny Boy rubbing juniper ashes on their thighs, and he performs it for every woman there. He is ecstatic: "Some thighs he gripped as if they were something wild and fleet like antelope and rabbits, and the women never flinched or hesitated because they believed the recovery of their clansister depended on them" (264). At the end of the ceremony, he hears Aunt Mamie say that she is feeling better, and Sonny Boy rides home with food and photographs of himself with the clanswomen.

This story comes at the end of *Storyteller* and offers a lighter version of artifice and ritual than we have seen in the other stories. Jennifer Browdy de Hernandez, however, is suspicious. She wonders if we as readers have not been duped: "The next page of the text, which is also the last page, is a big picture of Leslie Marmon Silko, smiling up wickedly at the camera. Is she too a trickster? Have we been lining up seriously in front of her, studying her stories reverentially, while she is laughing into her sleeve?"[13] I suspect Hernandez is correct as long as we understand that the nature of tricksters is to be seriously funny. There is certainly evidence of playfulness in *Storyteller,* and that playfulness translates nicely to readers unfamiliar with much of the background to the stories. *Storyteller* offers a remarkable blend of the serious and the playful, the tragic and the comic, and the political and the personal. They are all different strands in a spiderweb that captures not only the essence of life in Laguna but also the ways in which many of us imagine ourselves in story.

Chapter Five

Words and Images: *The Delicacy and Strength of Lace* and *Sacred Water*

The categories that shape artistic expression in Western culture are rarely able to contain the abundant aesthetics of Native American cultures. One of the great difficulties for nonnative scholars studying Native American literature or art is learning how to suspend, ignore, or modify the interpretive strategies that they bring to the "text" in order to experience the power of Native American expressions in their own terms. Like Leslie Marmon Silko, many Native American artists operate in a variety of genres and forms. In fact, by speaking with their own voices drawn from their own cultural and aesthetic experiences, Native American artists blur the boundaries that nonnative scholars and writers often assume. Native Americans also employ a political dimension consciously and conspicuously in the service of decolonialism. Silko in particular is adept at transgressing these artificial boundaries for the sake of the story. We have seen many times how she refuses to allow her work to be pigeon-holed in the structures of Western literary history and how she weaves her stories with strands of many kinds of materials.

One of Silko's primary interests is interaction between words and images, and this interest has led her to pursue some interesting projects. A good example of her willingness to experiment with this combination is the film she directed in 1980 with the help of Dennis Carr titled *Estoyehmuut and the Gunnadeyah* or *Arrowboy and the Destroyers*. Although the film never made it through production, the effort to make it shows a willingness on Silko's part to explore the visual medium in ways that would be uncomfortable for most writers. Even more risky perhaps was the creation of a one-act play of "Lullaby" that was adapted with Frank Chin. In the play the stories take on a third dimension by employing real people and a three-dimensional set. If stories do in fact have the power that she claims they do, then they should spill out of every genre and medium. In this chapter I examine two of Silko's works that fall outside the realm of traditional literature. *The Delicacy and Strength of Lace* is a collection of letters between Silko and poet James Wright and edited by Anne Wright, his wife.[1] *Sacred Water* is Silko's effort to create a book from start to finish using the technology she has in her home.[2]

The Delicacy and Strength of Lace

The Delicacy and Strength of Lace is the correspondence of two friends who are very different culturally but who share a love of language and stories that easily bridges their differences. Though they met only twice, Silko and Wright became dear friends through their letters, which concern everything from cocky roosters to the nature of language and life. Their first meeting was at a writer's conference in 1975, and they met again at Wright's hospital room just before he died. Their friendship became so special and Wright's death so painful that Silko has yet to read this book. She tells Donna Perry that when Anne Wright sent the manuscript for her review, she could not face it. After her friend Larry McMurtry read it for her, Silko wrote back to Wright and said, "Go ahead [and publish it]. I'm told it's very beautiful" (Perry, 332). These letters are intensely personal, humorous, and philosophical; moreover, they provide remarkable insights into the forces that shape Silko's writing and thinking. Although all of Silko's writings are personal, most are written in a public voice. *The Delicacy and Strength of Lace* offers readers a chance to hear a more private voice from a public storyteller.

The letters begin with an appropriately formal tone that also evidences sincere appreciation as James Wright feels compelled to share his recent experience of reading *Ceremony*. After struggling with a way to convey its effect upon him, he finally decides that "my very life means more to me than it would have meant if you hadn't written *Ceremony*" (3). He concludes by telling Silko that he is very happy that she is alive and writing books. Their letters display a mutual effort to speak candidly within the constraints of professional correspondence. Both writers, perhaps hindered by their reticence to draw too much upon a newly formed acquaintance, resort to disclaimers about their ability to say what they mean. It is Silko finally who breaks the ice by writing a long letter that contains a detailed story about roosters and their antics. At the end of the letter, she confesses that she never knows what will happen when she writes because certain people bring out certain stories, and in this letter she simply could not stop herself from writing about roosters. This confession leads to others about her reading habits and her feeling of being an outsider to the American writing community.

She also tells Wright that she trusts his voice as she does no other. Her trust in Wright leads her to send him some of her new poetry that appears in *Storyteller,* but it is clearly the rooster story that ignites the friendship. Perhaps it displays some risk on Silko's part, and if so, Wright responds in kind.

Wright responds by sharing a story about the loneliness of a friend whom he cheered up by visiting him unexpectedly. The lines separating the professional and the personal are clearly being blurred at this point. In his letter he notes that he is still processing *Ceremony* and remarks that he is trying to find a ceremony for his life. Silko's writings have become part of his personal ceremony of reading that occurs early in the mornings, and he writes to tell Silko that he is spending more and more time with her work. At the time her only published works were *Laguna Woman* and *Ceremony.* Of *Laguna Woman* Wright remarks: "It is curious how such a brief book has such enormous space in it, a space full of echoes and voices" (21−22), which is a fine description of the work. He goes on to describe her work as "abundant" as the seasons are abundant. Commenting upon the presence of pain in both their pasts, Wright notes that it is essential that the story of this pain and endurance be told. He indicates that for him no living writer understands the importance of stories the way Silko does. These generous and truthful comments from Wright no doubt invite Silko into a writing community of two and provide the storyteller with a context that, even though written, echoes that of a storytelling session in Laguna.

As Silko was corresponding with James Wright, she was working on two different projects: completing the writing and editing of *Storyteller* and producing the film *Estoyehmuut and the Gunnadeyah.* She often writes to Wright about the processes involved in creating a film and how those methods are different from writing. Film allows Silko to incorporate the landscape of the stories in ways other than through lengthy prose descriptions. Film has a unique ability to convey the landscape of the stories, even though it too is limited. "Translations of Laguna stories seem terribly blank on the printed page," she writes. The old stories are lean because they do not need to do this work of translation; the landscape is assumed by the storytellers and hearers, and there is no need to describe it in great detail. In writing the scripts for the film, she realizes that the final product may never appear. She says that "whatever the outcome, I will have written something interesting." She goes on to say that she thinks she needs to wean herself from the involved descriptions of the land that are necessary in fiction but not in film. At the same time, she recognizes that language has possibilities that visual media do not, namely, the ability to construct settings that are impossible to construct visually. She also recognizes that a simple scene change in film can do what requires lines of prose. These thoughts on the visual and verbal reveal much of what inspires Silko in her translation of the stories to the printed page.

Wright responds to Silko's comments about weaning herself from lengthy descriptions of the land as many of her readers might. He hopes that she is referring to her work on the film scripts, not to her writing style in general. Wright comments that it is those descriptions that drive the story, and in many ways they are the landscape telling its story. Silko picks up on this last observation and responds that such an evocation is exactly what she was hoping for in the telling of her stories. She seems relieved that she has allowed the land to tell its story without sounding like a transcendentalist. It is then that she mentions writing *Ceremony* in Alaska under difficult emotional and physical conditions. She comments: "I was so terribly devastated by being away from the Laguna Country that the writing was my way of re-making that place . . . for myself" (28). She likens writing to the creation of a sandpainting. Each painting is unique and directed toward the suffering individual. Symbols orient the person in a particular landscape, and after the individual has completed the ceremony, the sandpainting is destroyed. We recall that Tayo's healing was effected in good part by Betonie's sandpainting, which Tayo must live out beyond the borders of the painting itself. Silko tells Wright that words are like the symbols in a sandpainting: They orient the writer in this case.

Words are ideas, and Silko plays with the notion that Plato perhaps was right when he argued that ideas are more important than things. She explores this notion further with a story about the Cochiti Pueblo. After their lands were flooded by the Army Corps of Engineers, the Cochiti continued to visit their shrines and other sacred places because the idea of the place remained although the location itself was under water. She suggests that death functions the same way; at Laguna the dead are loved and love in return. The evidence of this love is that the family still feeds those who have passed on[3] by leaving them pinches of food, and the dead return the gifts by sending rain clouds or providing a feeling of closeness among the family members.[4] In this ironic discussion of death a year before James Wright learns he has cancer, Silko provides a remark that will be unknowingly prophetic for both of them. She writes to him in the same letter: "At Laguna, when someone dies, you don't 'get over it' by forgetting; you 'get over it' by *remembering,* and by remembering that you are aware that no person is ever truly lost or gone once they have been in our lives and loved us, as we have loved them" (29). Silko remembers Wright so much that she cannot read *The Delicacy and Strength of Lace* to this day; for her there is plenty of memory in her heart.

Related to these thoughts about ideas and place is a brief but instructive comment to Wright about David Hume. Silko is nothing if not well read, and she tells Wright that she has been reading David Hume because she understands him better than Plato. Her interest in Hume is in cause-and-effect, specifically in comparing Laguna notions with Western notions of the same. "Hume is refreshing," she tells Wright, and she admires him for his bravery and free thought in times that did not necessarily value these things. On one level Hume is one of the last names we would expect to hear from a Native American writer discussing her recent reading. On the other hand, it is not surprising that a Native American would learn the language of the dominant culture for the sake of survival and revolution. Silko knows and appreciates the Western tradition, even though she is keenly aware of the horrors it has produced. She reads Wittgenstein, Margaret Fuller, and Faulkner without apology.

After this exchange of letters, Anne and James Wright leave on a long trip through Europe that begins and ends with Paris and takes them through several cities. During this time Silko remains in Tucson except for a few weeks when she is in Seattle to teach at the University of Washington and at Vassar College for a writing workshop. As they travel to their various destinations, Silko and Wright become somewhat shorter in their responses, at times writing postcards rather than letters. The content of the letters has more to do with details of Wright's travels or happenings around Silko's home. The story of the rooster continues as Silko provides updates (he acquires two hens, for example). One day, however, Silko returns home to find the rooster gone and only a pile of feathers in its place. She eventually finds a few white feathers from the hens, but the conclusion is clear: The coyotes have come. The rooster that provided the story that inaugurated their friendship had finally met his end, although his feathers continued to blow in the wind for some time. Silko remarks: "He was a mean and dirty bird but we loved him in a strange sort of way. Our friends who had been pursued or jumped by the rooster find it difficult to appreciate our loss" (41). These thoughts lead her to speculate about love and why it is that we love things that are unlovable in ordinary terms. She decides that her 31 years have taught her that we are liable to love anything because "there are no limits to our love." The letter contains echoes of the short story "Uncle Tony's Goat," where one thing that is resolved at the end is whether Uncle Tony loves his goat or his nephew more. Silko displays the same sort of emotions in regard to her rooster, a "mean and dirty bird" that she was able to love and also to live without.

In Bruges, Belgium, Jim Wright comes across some shops that are selling lace. This discovery prompts him to think about lace, namely, that it is purely ornamental and serves no function in survival. The men and women who weave this lace, however, continue a trade that is part of an ancient tradition. In a moment of inspiration, the Wrights purchase some lace for Silko's birthday. It would become, like the rooster, an enduring but fragile symbol of a friendship spun by words. In fact, Silko immediately understands Wright's comment about the uselessness of lace and states that "that's the 'good' of the lace—that it is *no good* against bullets—something like the rooster who was *no* damn good at all, making him precious indeed" (46–47).

In these ruminations on "uselessness," Silko responds to a revelation from Wright about his reading of Spinoza. He recalls a profoundly difficult passage for him where the Jewish philosopher argues that humanity is unique and miraculous in its capacity to love, but even that miracle is not enough to ensure that an individual will be loved back, either by God or another human being. Not only is there no guarantee that we will be loved, according to Spinoza, but we also do not have the right to demand that we be loved in return for the love we give. Wright admits that this truth has been a hard thing for him to face, but he continues to confront it nonetheless. Silko writes back that she recalls Spinoza arguing the same point about good deeds, that we have no right to expect a good deed in return, and she writes that she plans to go to the library and read Spinoza again. The lace, the rooster, and Spinoza are all free associations that are not so free upon closer examination. The lace with its delicate nature and surprising strength is the perfect analog to the spider's web, which has the same qualities. The lace and the web, moreover, are profound symbols for the words that tie Silko and Wright together in friendship. The statement about the fragility and necessity of spoken language and the story by Ku'oosh in *Ceremony* is echoed here. The rooster is the ideal symbol of Spinoza's claim that we have no right to demand love, but we do have a right to receive it. Love, friendship, and words are delicate and strong, and like a spider's web, they are easily torn away. This poignant exchange about love and loss, expectations and gifts, and words and meaning is thrown into high relief by the reader's perspective from which we know Wright is soon to die. In retrospect, it appears that the two writers and friends anticipated a profound loss in the future, and they certainly experienced deep losses in the past. At the same time, they are keenly aware that the connection between them, consisting of words and stories, is vital and inviolable. Wright will remark in a later letter that "the important thing is to keep the *feeling* that the story has . . . the *feeling* one has of the story is what you must strive to bring forth faithfully" (70). Silko herself will write: "I am overwhelmed sometimes and feel a great deal of wonder at words, just simple words and how deeply we can touch each other with them" (74).

After the Wrights return to New York, James learns that he has cancer. The letter is short and to the point: He tells her he has it and that it is serious but not hopeless. The cancer is in the throat, and surgery will save his life but leave him with a diminished ability to speak, which is especially problematic because, unlike Silko, he is a full-time, tenured professor. Wright is clearly courageous and unsentimental as he tells Silko that he will find his way through these troubles and wants to share them with only his closest and dearest friends. "The tragic news belongs to you too," he tells her, and evokes the spirit of Spinoza in his understanding that no one can place demands upon life. Silko waits a few days before responding, and when she does, it is with a story from Laguna. Hugh Crooks was a man who came to Laguna in the 1920s and lived there at least until 1980 when this letter was written. Hugh Crooks is the man who will not die. He came to Laguna because he had tuberculosis and desired to wait out his final days in a drier climate. He waited and waited, but nothing happened. After he did not die, he began working around Laguna and ended up outliving many people who said that he would never make it because he got into so many physical disasters. The story is very detailed and runs for several pages, and as it is read the web is almost tangible as it spins itself around the grief and connects with other stories and people who suffer. There is a lot of humor in the story, and for the reader at least it provides a certain amount of levity that helps to contextualize the news of Wright's prognosis. Silko sums up her response herself when she writes: "You are a dear friend, Jim. In so many ways it was you who helped me through those difficult times last year. At times like these I often wish I had more to say, but somehow it comes out in a story" (102). After Silko visits him in the hospital when he is unable to speak, he writes to Anne Wright on a legal pad: "I

have the sense of a very fine, great person—a true beautiful artist"
(103). James Wright never got to read Silko's last letter to him, dated
one day before his death. In that letter she tells him: "In this place . . .
there never has been a time when you and I were not together. I cannot
explain this. Maybe it is the continuing or on-going of the telling,
telling in poetry and stories" (105).

   The Delicacy and Strength of Lace is a remarkably private dialogue
made public for the sake of the story. Although Silko has yet to read this
book, she certainly remembers the intimate nature of the letters and the
friendship. More personal in many ways than an autobiography, *The
Delicacy and Strength of Lace* offers readers a revealing dialogue on writing
by two of the nation's most passionate and articulate voices. Readers
interested in Silko's motivations and influences will do well to listen in
on the dialogue between her and James Wright as they weave a delicate
yet strong web of words that constitute a friendship so obviously beyond
words.

Sacred Water

Sacred Water is Silko's first (and so far only) attempt at publishing. The
first editions of this book were printed, sewed, glued, and distributed by
Silko under the imprint of her own Flood Plain Press. As we saw in the
biographical sketch, the desire to take on the responsibility of a book
from beginning to end is one that she has had since the fifth grade. The
early editions, she admits with some pride, look like a child produced
them.[5] *Sacred Water* is the essay on water that Silko mentions in *Yellow
Woman and A Beauty of the Spirit,* and it consists of nonfiction prose that
flows around her own photographs of the area around her Tucson home.
These black-and-white photographs have been copied on a home copy
machine: "I take my photographs and print them on a laser copying
machine in the 'photo' mode; the resulting image is more stark and
abstract than a traditional photographic print which tends to dominate
the page regardless of the text" (80). The book tours for *Almanac of the
Dead* had made her weary of the publishing culture, so she did not discuss the possibility of publishing *Sacred Water* with her editor. Instead,
she published the book herself. One wonders why she was not more
interested in the Blake class she took in graduate school; they obviously
have much in common.

   The very existence of *Sacred Water* is an excellent example of the issues
that drive Silko's work. She finds her authorial identity in the transgres-

sion of the boundaries of the book and transgresses further by crossing the borders that define the roles of author, printer, and publisher. In this book she is able to explore on her own terms the dialogue of visual and verbal that fascinates her and provides an interesting backdrop to the history of communication and aesthetics in Western culture. Other authors and artists do this as well, such as Blake, but Silko has her own interest and angle on the issue. In the author's note, she argues that photographs depend upon words just as words depend upon images. As an example she uses the images of the overturned, empty Kuwaiti incubators during the Gulf War. Without words the images are ambivalent and without context. The media, however, immediately provided a context in the form of a story about Iraqi soldiers dumping the Kuwaiti babies out of these incubators. After the war we hear another story and understand that we have been deceived. Photographs, then, are not independent of stories, and Silko's interest in *Sacred Water* is not to supplement the photographs with the "true" story behind them but instead to run two stories at the same time: the visual and the verbal. The dialogue that emerges from this juxtaposition will depend upon the story readers provide for the photographs as well as those that intersect the text. Silko deliberately wants to distance the photographs from the text in order to create a space for interpretation to play. She also notes that because she is writer, printer, and publisher, the text itself evolves: "When I see a word or phrase or a punctuation . . . which I don't like, I simply change it the next time I run-off a hundred copies of *Sacred Water*" (83). Silko wants to release readers from the trance that a stable visual image, whether a photograph or a text, creates. Theorists such as Walter Ong and Marshall McLuhan have described the effects of print upon the human psyche and interpretation in such terms, and they are also careful to point out that oral cultures, such as the Pueblo, tend to view language and stories as much more fluid than Westerners who are hypnotized by print.[6] In *Sacred Water,* as in her other work, Silko attempts to apply the fluidity of language to the "text" of photographs and prose. The lesson she hopes we will learn is the same one that Betonie teaches Tayo, namely, that change is not dangerous, only the inability to change is.

The current editions of *Sacred Water* are bound like other books; that is, they do not have the look and feel of the earlier versions. On the cover is a color drawing by Silko herself that depicts rain clouds and other items related to the rain such as flowers. Throughout most of the book, the stark photographs have their own page while the text appears on separate pages. For two pages near the middle of the book, text and photograph share the page, although the photograph spans the length of the two pages. There is quite a bit of white space throughout, which adds to the starkness of the photographs as well as of the writing. The nonfiction prose that accompanies the photographs is reminiscent of certain sections of *Storyteller,* where Silko takes on the role of storyteller at one remove. She tells stories about the telling of stories, and all these tales concern rain or water. There is a sense of free association that makes the text smooth and graceful as it snakes around the images. Because there are no divisions in the book, it seems unfair to break it up into sections, but there are themes that seem to surface for several pages at times.

In the first photographs, clouds dominate, whereas landscape shots appear more frequently in the middle and latter pages. The only photograph that is not of the sky in the first 13 pages is of a pool of water that reflects the clouds above it. The text in these first pages is largely concerned with memories of childhood and water. Silko tells us that one of her first lessons in interpretation was learning to read the sky for changes in the weather. She also recalls that with the fat, dark clouds came the rain smell that figures prominently in *Laguna Woman.* There were prohibitions against harming frogs because they are children of the rain clouds. Water was special to Grandmother Anaya because she was a member of the water clan, which meant that a large pot of water stood at the head of her grave at her funeral. Springs are especially sacred because they are places where the world below emerges into the fifth world to nourish it with its abundant life. In the Southwest, water takes on a prominence that is hard for easterners to imagine. Because life depends on water, images and rituals tend to focus on water and its incarnations in clouds and rivers. "The Man to Send Rain Clouds" offers a good example of the nature of water for the Pueblos. It dominates the imagination because without it there is no life.

In the next pages we find a series of photographs of snakes swimming in water. The text describes the origin of Ma ah shra true ee, the sacred messenger, and how he lived at the lake for which Laguna was named until jealousy caused him to go back to mother creator below. After that the lake dried up. We have heard stories like this one before, specifically, in *Ceremony,* in which the corn mother retreats to the fourth world when her altar is neglected, and Reed Woman does the same. Also in *Ceremony* mother earth herself withholds water because of the rule of the destroyers as evidenced in the World War and the witchery that it conjures up.

Snakes are often associated with life in non-Western cultures because they shed their skin and continue on. The image of the snake eating its tail is a common one in Eastern cultures, where it signifies timelessness, among other things.[7] We also learn that petroglyphs of coiled snakes were signs of a spring nearby with the head of the snake pointing toward the water source. Apparently, the Spaniards took this symbol to be an indicator of hidden treasure, such as gold. Silko writes that they misunderstood because "fresh water is the treasure" (29).

The middle portion of the book concerns stories of the way rain shapes the lives of people at home. One of the effects of living on the edge of the village at Laguna is that the edge is also below the village near the San Jose River. The river provides the setting for the Yellow Woman stories and the place for mixed-bloods like the Marmons. Silko recalls the water from the summer rainstorms rushing past her home and the family worrying about the adobe walls, which melt in rain, and the cellar, which Robert Marmon insisted upon building because homes in his native Ohio all had cellars. A flooded cellar meant crumbling adobe walls, so the family watched the rain and the runoff with some anxiety. A photograph, looking down toward the narrow space between two walls, accompanies the stories of the Marmon home and may well be a photograph of a cellar. It could just as easily be a photograph taken from the top of a mesa and looking down into a narrow canyon; the scale is ambiguous. The concern about the house was mitigated by the elaborate constructions of a neighbor who managed to build rock dams along the roadway that directed the runoff toward his fruit trees, corn, and squash. Silko recalls that his engineering was unknown for some time because the rocks were inconspicuously blended in with the land-scape. After this man died and the dams were not maintained, the runoff became so bad that government engineers spent a significant amount of money to manage the runoff with the same result as her neighbor. There is, of course, an obvious implication to this story, namely, that respecting the land and the water is effective because it provides mutual enrichment. The water was controlled by means appro-priate to the landscape (rocks), and the result was a blending of culture and nature at no expense to the people.

The thoughts about rain and home bring her to discuss roofs, and although there are no photographs of roofs, there are images of both cis-terns and dry washes as if to juxtapose the way humans deal with water and the way mother earth does. An early childhood memory of Silko's has to do with the roof of her adobe home leaking down the walls and the water looking like melted chocolate. One can easily imagine the child's perspective and see the delicious colors of the water on the pink adobe. She also discusses catchment systems on roofs in Tucson and Alaska that provide water when wells and reservoirs do not. Beside a photograph of a flower blooming in a pool of water, the text tells of the seductive danger of pools in southern Arizona, where a number of drownings occur every year. The message is subtle but clear: Water is dangerous even when contained.

After this discussion of roofs and rain, Silko describes at great length the water around her home, specifically a pool that provided animals with a source of water and furnished a home for numerous singing toads. The toads are eventually killed by the careless children of a visitor and by his dog, and then other dogs surround a deer who has come to drink and end up trampling the plants around the pond. After these events a mysterious red algae appears that cannot be killed. No animals or plant life can coexist with this stubborn and prodigious new inhabitant. Water hyacinths finally become the heroes of this story since they are the only thing that can beat back the encroaching algae. As the water hyacinths flourish, the pool returns to life. This story leads Silko to think about the sacred and hallucinogenic datura plant. Also known as jimson weed, this plant will absorb plutonium and become radioactive in the place of the soil in which it lives. Silko suggests that the datura recognizes all water as sacred. In fact, the last line of text reads: "Whatever may become of us human beings, the Earth will bloom with hyacinth purple and the white blossoms of the datura" (76). This story provides interesting reading for *Ceremony* and *Almanac of the Dead,* adumbrating as it does the perdurability of mother earth against any and all attacks against her, even the attack of nuclear destruction. The earth will survive; it has its own mechanisms for doing so. It is we who are in danger of extinction.

A close reading of the texts in *Sacred Water* reveals that Silko is once again spinning a web of words, only this time she is using images as well. She is careful not to allow the images simply to supplement the text or the text to be overwhelmed by the images. The images and the prose are two strands that we are allowed to connect on our own without any interpretive instructions. The result is a book that is round rather than flat, open rather than closed, and dialogic rather than monologic. A story in the author's note illustrates this notion well. Silko tells us that she received two letters from concerned professors who listed the errors in the first edition of the book. Silko readily admits that she is a terrible speller, typist, and proofreader, and this is why she will never publish any other author under the imprint of Flood Plain Press. In a playful move, she quotes a portion of one of her letters to one of these earnest professors. First of all, she incorporates the professor into the oral tradition by explaining that the collaborative spirit that points out errors is a part of the storytelling culture at Laguna. She then points out that "It was Noah Webster who sought to standardize spellings, pronunciations, and usages in the U.S. so that the regional and ethnic differences among the 13 original states might be minimized. Webster's first dictionary was intended to 'homogenize' this country" (84).

These comments are instructive in several ways: They provide another glimpse into Silko's persona, they display her remarkable wit, and they offer insight into her theoretical disposition. As to the latter, we may find similar ideas about the function of language in theorists like Mikhail Bakhtin, who argues that there are two poles in the life of language. Centripetal forces attempt to freeze language into a static center, whereas centrifugal forces diffuse meaning outward into different discourses or, as Silko might say, stories. Bakhtin terms this latter force *heteroglossia,* and it is this direction that Silko champions in her letter. Centripetal forces tend toward homogenization; centrifugal forces move toward difference. I do not want to imply that Silko is one-sided in Bakhtin's formulation; on the contrary, she recognizes both poles in the life of language. Her contention is that in the end, centrifugal forces win out because to grow is to change, and stasis is related to death. *Sacred Water* is a material manifestation of this fact of language and life. It works to expand the possibilities of stories, to allow other stories to emerge from words and images as it values story itself above all things. Stories are like sacred water; we cannot live without them.

Chapter Six
Almanac of the Dead:
The Politics of Time

Almanac of the Dead is a watershed in the Leslie Marmon Silko corpus.[1] Longer by 500 pages than any of her other works, *Almanac* serves as the culmination of Silko's research, thought, anger, and her attempt to achieve some form of justice for indigenous people. We have already seen how this novel, her second, dominated her life for a decade during a time when American politics (under Presidents Ronald Reagan and George Bush) and Arizona politics (under Governor Evan Mecham) merged in frightening ways, especially in their sustained attack upon the disenfranchised that was disguised as economic patriotism. This political context is important to understanding the novel, but it must also be noted that the injustices of the eighties are, in Silko's mind, simply the latest incarnation of an evil that is nearly 500 years old. As it sweeps through the history of the Americas, the novel conveys much more than the protest of one woman or even one people. *Almanac* is in fact a legal document written by a storyteller: "This is my 763-page indictment for five hundred years of theft, murder, pillage, and rape. So is *Almanac* long? Sure, for federal indictments are long. The one returned against Charles Keating, who took one billion dollars just in one savings and loan in Arizona, is long. And mine is a little more interesting reading than a straight-on legal indictment" (Perry, 327). Silko never stopped being interested in legal issues relevant to indigenous people, and this novel is an expression of the same passion that propelled her into law school. *Almanac* stands as an epic and eloquent statement of justice denied and reclaimed for the dispossessed of three continents and half a millennium.

Whereas the political and legal dimensions of the novel are clear and detailed, the moral dimension is more subtle. The characters in *Almanac,* whether native or European, embody a decadence that is rarely matched in American fiction. From the Tucson judge whose sexual pleasures are confined to his basset hounds, to a homeless man who kills other homeless men just as they are ejaculating into his mouth, to a sadistic drug dealer who leaves his lovers with suicide kits, Silko's second novel is a parade of the worst characters that Western culture can produce. These characters are both native and white, and few classes of people are spared in the catalogue of contemporary perversions and crimes that is *Almanac*. The common thread that ties these characters together is their fascination with and manipulation of death in all its forms. Silko recalls feeling sorry for readers of *Ceremony* who waited eagerly for nearly 15 years for another novel: "Oh no, these dear little people that love *Ceremony*, what's going to happen to them when they get sucked into the maelstrom of *Almanac*? In Seattle a man told me he thought *Almanac* was affecting his sanity, and finally I just said, 'I hope it won't harm you, or if you think it is, then stop' " (Perry, 332–33). Only a dogged reading of this demanding almanac of death, destruction, and evil can reveal the calculated horror and despair that permeates the universe of *Almanac of the Dead*.

Despite the depravity of its characters, *Almanac* is not a gratuitous display of perversion and decadence; on the contrary, the novel elicits moral judgment from its readers. The very fact that we know that these characters are horrific reinforces our own sense of right while it marks how far we have deviated from that sense as a society. *Almanac* judges Euro-American culture by its own standards, and that culture falls tragically short. At the same time, Native American values gradually emerge from their entanglement with colonial culture to offer some sense of hope for anyone who loves and respects the earth. *Almanac of the Dead* is a moral statement as much as anything else, and it calls us to judge the society that we all have made through greed and ecological apathy. Silko bares all, pulls no punches, and leaves us exhausted from the sheer force of our own moral outrage. That anger is a function of her stripping away the veneer of ambiguity that covers the moral fabric of America and showing us the ugly acts underneath. *Almanac* is the antithesis of morality by obfuscation; instead, it offers us a clear choice between creation and destruction.

When Kim Barnes asked Silko about the audiences for her fiction, she responded that she was working on "this new novel" that is "long and complex to the point of being foolhardy" (47). She goes on to say: "I don't want to write something that the MLA [Modern Language Association] will want. I want something that will horrify the people at the MLA" (47–48). Although she says that she is only halfway serious, the point is well taken and should be considered by anyone who is attempting to analyze this novel. Following general themes is possible but sacrifices the particulars of character development and the many individual stories that make up *Almanac*. On the other hand, because there are so many characters, plot lines, and settings, paying attention to the particulars in the novel is practically impossible. There is a point to this confusion: Literary criticism, whether traditional or contemporary, depends upon certain assumptions about time and place, namely, that time is stable and apolitical, and the landscape is a palimpsest for culture.

Time and place are precisely those concepts that Silko wants to reimagine in *Almanac of the Dead* by subverting Western notions of time and place and allowing indigenous ideas to emerge from the chaos of Euro-American decadence. She remarks: "The way time is computed in Western European cultures is completely political. Colonialists always want time and history not to go back very far. . . . Time is totally political—especially when they are on that mother ground and especially when it's such a short period of time, where somebody living today could have talked to somebody who had talked to somebody who actually was at the scene of some of these events" (329). *Almanac of the Dead* is an extended conversation of somebody who talked with somebody else who was at the scene for the past 500 years. As such it creates a network of people, events, and stories that mythologizes time and space as the Mayan almanacs did.[2] Only one of the many plot lines that drive the book concerns the recovery of a lost almanac that was handed down by Lecha and Zeta's grandmother Yoeme.[3] The almanac is a set of notebooks with cryptic references to people and events both past and future. Lecha's task is to decipher these notebooks, and in doing so she creates different understandings of time and space that swallow up our ordinary notions of them. Silko's work, then, attacks the very ground upon which we stand as readers and asks us to rethink the way we imagine time and space.

Almanac frustrates attempts to interpret it with the tools of close reading. In that sense it is difficult if not impossible to replicate the reader's experience to a satisfactory degree. Even those who have read the novel have difficulty talking about it to others because it deluges readers with information and new ways of interpreting that knowledge. Given these constraints, I do not attempt to elucidate the reader's experience any more than I have already done in these preliminary remarks. Instead, I discuss the opening and closing books and then follow two of the most important threads found throughout: technology and time.

Tucson—The Beginning

There are at least 65 different characters in *Almanac of the Dead,* and all of them have stories to tell that relate to the larger story of the novel.

The image of the spiderweb appears here as well, as the map at the beginning shows. Characters, cities, and events are connected by lines on the map, and at the center of the web is Tucson, Arizona, which a caption tells us is "home to an assortment of speculators, confidence men, embezzlers, lawyers, judges, police and other criminals, as well as addicts and pushers, since the 1880s and the Apache wars." The characters fit generally into the places in which we initially find them, but there is also quite a bit of movement as they are slowly orchestrated into an apocalyptic symphony. The places, whether cities or general areas, make up most of the topics of 19 books that comprise the novel. Like the ancient Mayan almanacs, these books parse the stories into self-contained units but also provide some sense of relation among the stories. The 19 books themselves are divided among six "parts" named the United States, Mexico, Africa, the Americas, the Fifth World, and finally "One World, Many Tribes." Book one (Tucson) of the first part (the United States of America) sets the stage for some of the most important events in the novel and introduces us to some of the major figures. Book one (Prophecy) of the last part (One World, Many Tribes) brings the strands of the novel together in one final scene for which the setting is Tucson. Many of the characters found in the opening book reappear in the closing one.

Almanac of the Dead opens with a provocative scene. In a familiar and comfortable setting, the kitchen, some of the oddest characters in American fiction appear. We meet Zeta first, who is standing at the stove over a simmering brown liquid in a blue enamel pot. The liquid is not food but dye "the color of dried blood," and Zeta is not a housewife preparing dinner for her adoring brood but the director, with her nephew Ferro, of a vast smuggling operation from Mexico that trades in drugs, arms, and people. Her sister, Lecha, is in the kitchen with them and has just returned to the Tucson ranch with Seese, a young woman in search of her child who hopes to use Lecha's psychic gifts to find her son. Lecha abandoned Ferro in Zeta's kitchen when he was one week old, and he has hated her ever since. Now Lecha sits in a wheelchair and waits for her early-evening Demerol, which is administered by her "nurse" Seese. Lecha and Zeta are twins, and they are spending their 60th birthday absorbed in their own devious plots while they share the same well-fortified house. Lecha is really there to translate the other almanac, the one that has not been appropriated by white culture and that has been handed down by their grandmother Yoeme. We are treated to portions of this almanac throughout, although some of it is too cryptic to allow us to decipher it for ourselves.

When Ferro suggests that Lecha and he are respectively the "old and the new blood," Zeta confirms it by nodding and saying, "Old age." She then jokingly suggests that she is dyeing her clothes black because she does not want to be visible at night. Lecha says, "Like a witch!" and laughs at the joke. This exchange provokes a response from Paulie, Ferro's sycophantic partner. Paulie comments that in prison dark colors are not allowed as they aid in night escapes. Zeta keeps Paulie around because he knows nothing else besides them and prison and thus makes a useful helper who cannot be tempted but can be threatened. Ferro both uses and abuses him, but Paulie stays around regardless and does whatever Ferro asks. After Seese finishes with the Demerol shot, Lecha becomes talkative. Surveying the kitchen scene, which includes pistols, shotguns, cartridges, and needles, but no food, Lecha proclaims: "The Devil's kitchen doesn't look this good" (20). Her description is well founded. Ferro is "coiled tighter than a mad snake," and they are all in the kitchen because of recent developments that we are not immediately privy to but have the air of evil. Sterling, a hired man from Laguna, is "in training for a special assignment," but we are not told what that might be; in fact, Sterling himself has been told very little.

This initial scene sets the stage for the frightening characters of *Almanac* to appear, indeed many of them are already in the kitchen. The language is as cryptic as the characters' words, and the atmosphere is one of dread and danger. The hatred that this "family" feel toward one another is palpable even in the first few paragraphs. For example, Ferro, upon observing his mother's ritual injection, offers the interpretation that the needle "slips in like a lover's prick and shoots the dope in white and hot." He thinks that Lecha, his mother, wants them all to watch her, but "*he* doesn't watch junky orgasms, not even for his *own* mother." After these comments he jumps up and runs outside while Paulie remains alert in case he is called.

While bloodlines connect Lecha, Zeta, and Ferro, the two "adopted" family members provide some sense of balance. Seese is a character who draws sympathy. She is a mother in search of her child and is willing to do almost anything to find him. Seese, however, is no innocent. Her past is sordid and includes a bad drug habit. Sterling is even more likable. An affable man who minds his own business and tries to help Seese, he has been unfairly banished from Laguna because of difficulties with a film crew whom he was to keep out of sacred areas near the uranium mine. His personal hobbies border on the bizarre, but that is a relative term in the world of *Almanac*.

The remainder of the first book concerns Sterling, and he becomes what Silko calls the "moral center" of the novel: "He's kind of all of us. Sterling was always trying to fix things up for people. He knew that it was a dangerous and bad world. My friend Larry McMurtry said that Sterling was his favorite character, and couldn't there be more of Sterling? And probably there could have been. But maybe there will be more Sterling in some other place, I don't know. He is a messenger, finally, too" (Perry, 330). Sterling is also very much like Silko. He is marginalized by his tribe, just as Silko was by being a mixed breed, interested in the law, as is Silko, and believes in the possibilities of creation rather than the portents of destruction. He is also a model for the reader as she examines the nature of time and space: "Whatever was coming would not necessarily appear right away; it might not arrive for twenty or even a hundred years. Because the old ones paid no attention to white man's time. But Sterling had never dreamed that one day his own life would be changed forever because of that mine. Those old folks had been right all along. The mine had destroyed Sterling's life without Sterling's ever setting foot near the acres of ruined earth at the open pit" (35). Sterling is a lightning rod for the evil in *Almanac;* he discharges some of the tension built up by the other characters by virtue of being someone with whom we can identify and sympathize. We wonder with him about the other ways of imagining time and space, and we are appalled with him as he contemplates the society around him.

Sterling's exile from Laguna is the result of his allowing a Hollywood movie crew to film the sacred snake at the uranium mine. Eighty years before Sterling's crime small stone idols that were given to the people by the Kachina spirits on their migration south disappeared from a kiva altar at a time when anthropologists were offering rewards for such items. The narrative moves from Sterling's recollection of his banishment to a story within a story, modeled on those forms in both *Ceremony* and *Storyteller,* that recounts the theft and discovery of the stone idols. This story within the story provides a synopsis of the native disposition in the novel and offers a counter to the opening scene in the infernal kitchen. The tale of the stone idols reflects the rising of all things native that will converge at the end of the novel, which is also the end of "time." After years of searching and employing diviners to locate the idols, the Laguna get word from one of the northern Pueblos to look in a museum outside Santa Fe. A delegation is dispatched that includes the old cacique and an interpreter.[4] In the early spring, while snow still covers the tops of the mountains, the delegation arrives in Santa Fe, and the interpreter goes inside to inquire about the idols as the others, including the old cacique, wait around a small fire. The assistant curator informs the interpreter that they have "two lithic pieces of that description," and the Lagunas file in to look. The scene is a poignant one, and the people are filled with both shock and anger to the point where they are speechless:

> The delegation walked past the display cases slowly and in silence. But when they reached the glass case in the center of the vast hall, the old cacique began to weep, his whole body quivering from old age and the cold. He seemed to forget the barrier glass forms and tried to reach out to the small stone figures lying dreadfully unwrapped. The old man kept bumping his fingers against the class case until the assistant curator became alarmed. The Laguna delegation later recounted how the white man had suddenly looked around at all of them as if he were afraid they had come to take back everything that had been stolen. In that instant white man and Indian both caught a glimpse of what was yet to come. (33)

As in the opening scene of the novel, this incident portends drastic changes in the way the balances of power will shift in time. The account of the stone idols sets in motion one of the major plots of the novel, which is the reconstitution of native peoples through the reclamation of the land. This plot runs simultaneously with the other major plot, which is the dissolution of the death cultures throughout the world. In this scene and in Sterling's overall story within the novel, these two lines intersect. The interpreter informs the curator that the museum is in possession of stolen property according to white law because "not even an innocent buyer got title of ownership to stolen property" (33). The Lagunas, moreover, can produce witnesses that will provide detailed descriptions of the "little grandparents." What the curator sees as lithic objects are to the Laguna actual beings shaped by the hands of the kachina spirits. When the curator explains that these objects were donated by a distinguished patron whose reputation is beyond reproach and that the delegation will have to return when the head curator returns, the members of the delegation raise their voices and explain that they have already traveled a great distance. Seeing the potential for a dangerous conflict, the curator escapes to the office and suggests that they hire a lawyer. The war captain lingers to memorize all the stolen objects he can see in the room.

In other novels this description might evoke the sense of loss that many Americans feel at the "disappearance" of native cultures. In

Almanac of the Dead, this story serves to foreshadow what is already underway: the reclamation of the land by indigenous peoples all over the western hemisphere. As Euro-American culture begins to fall, indigenous cultures begin to rise and shake off the oppressive structures that keep them disempowered and disenfranchised. There are countless examples throughout the novel that depict this phenomenon. One that is relevant to the story of the stone idols and brings us back to Sterling is the story of the uranium mine near Laguna. We will see that this place will play an important role in Sterling's life as well as in the plot of the novel. The great stone snake appears here over 30 years after the creation in 1949 of a mine near Laguna. The old ones had resisted allowing the whites to cut into mother earth so close to the emergence place, but in the end they had no choice, and the mine ended up creating some jobs for the people. Still the older people predicted that there would be consequences for "this desecration, this crime against all living things."[5] The predictions of the old ones, whether in Laguna or in the almanacs from Central America, will come true in their own time: "Whatever was coming would not necessarily appear right away; it might not arrive for twenty or even a hundred years. Because these old ones paid no attention to white man's time" (35).

White man's time is precisely what is questioned in *Almanac,* and we will see later that the subversion of that sense of time is encoded in the narrative itself. The very fact that there are so many narratives that span so much time moves us out of our comfortable notions of the regularity of time and history and into a world where time is tied to events and the rhythms of the earth, rather than to some abstract register. For example, Sterling reflects upon the Great Depression of 1929 when he was a boy. In Laguna the depression is not remembered at all because the Laguna had no money in the banks to lose and no mortgages on property. What they do remember is the winters of the early thirties being mild and wet and producing plentiful harvests and fat game: "The Laguna people had heard something about 'The Crash.' But they remembered 'The Crash' as a year of bounty and plenty for the people" (41). As Silko points out, time is political, and in *Almanac* she offers a new politics of time.

The people of Laguna are unable to separate the stories of the idols and the filming of the stone snake, even though the theft of the stone idols had occurred several decades before. The people know that time has passed, of course, and feel despair at realizing that soon there would be no one left who could remember actually seeing the stone idols laid out upon their altar. They are not, however, trapped in this one dimension of time; the Laguna traditionals understand the larger register of time kept by mother earth, who will outlive everything: "All of that happened seventy years before, but Sterling knew that seventy years was nothing—a mere heartbeat at Laguna" (34). Thus the desecration of the great stone snake by the film crew seemed like a continuation of the tragedy of the stolen idols. It does not matter to the Lagunas that the members of the film crew did not understand what it was they were seeing. The elders disagree with Sterling's position that, since the film crew is ignorant of the story, the secret is still intact. The simultaneity of the theft of the stone idols will not allow the Laguna to separate the two events. Both the theft and the filming are part of one story, a story that spans years. In the world of this story, the sacrilege is painfully present.

The novel continues to plot two different lines on its historical graph. In one, Euro-American culture is heading downward into the implosion that is inevitable for those who deal in death and greed. In the other, indigenous cultures that respect and honor the earth are rising. Betonie tells Tayo in *Ceremony* that there are balances and harmonies always shifting. Throughout *Almanac* we see this happen in various places and times and in several characters. Whether it is Mexico, Africa, Alaska, or Tucson, the tide is turning back toward the earth and creation. The reign of "Death-Eye Dog" is coming to an end. By the end of the novel we are ready to see this happen and are eager for the pattern to emerge.

Book One: Prophecy—The End

Tucson is the center of the world in *Almanac*. The opening book is set there as is this final one, and much of the action in between these two books concerns this city. The last book of the novel brings together the many different plot lines, characters, and prophecies that appear throughout. After plowing through 700 pages of torture, murder, government plots, ancient prophecies, revisionist history, and traditional tales, the reader (at least the nonnative reader) is ready for closure. The tension that Silko builds up is palpable, and by the final book most readers are seeking some release to that tension. The stage is set for an apocalyptic convergence of the two plot lines of Euro-American dissolution and indigenous reconstitution. The particular setting is a meeting in a Tucson resort of a variety of characters and their agendas that is called the International Holistic Healers Convention. Like almost everything else in this novel, the convention is a front for all sorts of devious and criminal activities. It also serves as a focus for the resurgence of native peoples since characters who support this resurgence directly or indirectly play prominent roles. Among these characters are the Barefoot Hopi, a political revolutionary and cultural hero, and Wilson Weasel Tail, a poet-lawyer who can incite both whites and natives to action and remorse.

Angelita, a Marxist revolutionary, is at the convention on behalf of the Mexican uprising and to bring a message from the twins, El Feo and Wacah (who is also Tacho in previous books), who are marching north from Mexico with a multitude to reclaim the land. Wacah and El Feo operate according to the orders of the sacred macaws, which means that they are not allowed to ride in automobiles or helicopters. They cannot, therefore, attend the convention but have asked Angelita to speak on their behalf. She is to invite the conventioneers to join the walk north: "It was only necessary to walk with the people and let go of all the greed and the selfishness in one's heart. One must be able to let go of a great many comforts and all things European; but the reward would be peace and harmony with all living things. All they had to do was return to Mother Earth. No more blasting, digging, or burning" (710). The message the twins want to convey to the healers is that they should be prepared for the changes, but "the changes might require another hundred years, until the Europeans had been outnumbered and the people retook the land peacefully." Angelita, however, is not interested in waiting another hundred years; she wants to hasten the revolution by means of violence. Known as "the meat hook" and La Escapia, Angelita is "the crazy Cuban from the coast" and a dangerous woman. She explains Marx and Engels to Mexican villages and helps them to revolt: "Marx understood what tribal people had always known: the maker of a thing pressed part of herself or himself into each object made" (520). Her lover, El Feo, fears her as much as he does anyone and with good reason. One of her speeches to the villagers ends with the execution of her comrade from Cuba—Bartolomeo—because he "has no use for indigenous history." Janet St. Clair describes Angelita well: "Champion of communitarian principles and gynocratic reclamation of the land for the chosen people, La Escapia is in fact a fascist leader of a fundamentalist jihad, sacrificing civility and polity in a war for power and identity, manipulating the masses into effecting her will and ruthlessly silencing those who challenge her unacknowledged autocracy."[6]

The narrative proceeds from Angelita's perspective to Lecha's, and Lecha is remembering the first time she encountered the poet-lawyer Wilson Weasel Tail, whom Lecha met on a talk show during which he lost control and began a diatribe that was memorable for its rage and brilliance. Part of his ravings include a fact that is not a little auto-biographical of Silko herself. His talk is peppered with poetry, and he relates that he abandoned law school when he realized that the deck was stacked against the poor. "All that is left is the power of poetry," he says. Wilson is to give the first address at the convention, and Lecha is eager to hear him again. Contemplating Wilson's program note that promises to teach the conventioneers how to summon up ghosts shifts Lecha's attention to the question of who has spiritual possession of the Americas. Her immediate response to herself is that it is certainly not the Christians. As the stories begin to telescope into the past, the narrative shifts to Lecha and Zeta's grandmother Yoeme. Though prohibited from casting aspersions on Christianity, Yoeme did so when Lecha and Zeta's mother was not in sight. Yoeme takes great delight in showing the girls how the mask of righteousness had slipped off the face of Christianity before the Spanish ships arrived in the Americas. Ordinary people learned that the church was a cannibal feeding off the flesh of its own. Yoeme offers the girls a revisionist history of the grand explorations of the sixteenth century:

> Christianity might work on other continents and with other human beings; Yoeme did not dispute those possibilities. But from the beginning in the Americas, the outsiders had sensed their Christianity was somehow inadequate in the face of the immensely powerful and splendid spirit beings who inhabited the vastness of the Americas. The Europeans had not been able to sleep soundly on the American continents, not even with a full military guard. They had suffered from nightmares and frequently claimed to see devils and ghosts. Cortes's men had feared the medicine and the procedures they had brought with them from Europe might lack power on New World soil; almost immediately, the wounded Europeans had begun to dress their wounds in the fat of slain Indians. (718)

Lecha is not seduced by Yoeme's vision of Christianity until she begins to work as a psychic and sees for herself the terror that white people feel despite their education and affluence. They named their sense of loss different things, but she knew that what was missing was a connection with the earth. In their fear of illness and change, "they sought to control death by becoming killers themselves."

Finally the convention speeches begin, and the narrative shifts back to the present. Wilson Weasel Tail's address to the convention is a wide-ranging diatribe that includes native chants, his own poetry, and a sub-version of anthropological and historical interpretations of the Ghost Dance. The Ghost Dance was a nineteenth-century religious movement among Native Americans across the country that predicted the end of the white culture and a return of the buffalo and of those who had died at the hands of the colonizers. Many of the participants wore shirts that were supposed to protect them from the bullets of the cavalry. The movement ended with the massacre at Wounded Knee in December 1890. Weasel Tail offers a corrective to this interpretation, and like other correctives in the novel, it involves reimagining our sense of time. He notes that anthropologists declare that the Ghost Dance disappeared because it did not produce immediate results (the Europeans did not vanish). Weasel Tail says that the misinterpretation comes in the form of white anthropologists believing that the shirts, which were of the spirit world, would offer protection from the bullets of the everyday world: "The ghost shirts gave the dancers spiritual protection while the white men dreamed of shirts that repelled bullets because they feared death" (722). The real meaning of the Ghost Dance was to reunite the living with the spirits of their ancestors. In that sense the Ghost Dance has never ended, and the novel itself can be seen to fit into Weasel Tail's schema. Although it may be called by other names, the people have continued to dance and attempted to be reunited with their ancestors: "Throughout the Americas, from Chile to Canada, the people have never stopped dancing; as the living dance, they are joined again with all our ancestors before them, who cry out, who demand justice, and who call the people to take back the Americas!" (724).

Among the many characters assembled at the International Holistic Healers Convention are a group of ecological activists who are working with the Barefoot Hopi to effect the release of mother earth from her bondage. The group are called the Eco-Warriors or Green Vengeance, and they give their lives for the earth. Before the Barefoot Hopi speaks, one of the eco-warriors provides a videotape that details the collapse of Glen Canyon Dam on the Colorado River. The tape records the group's preparations as they arrange explosives and pack them into a backpack. What the authorities call "structural failure" is in fact the result of a sui-cidal mission on the part of Green Vengeance to free the Colorado River. The tape shows the warriors disappearing under the pieces of the dam and the torrent of water that was aching to break free. A second warrior speaks to the convention about the stakes involved in the war to liberate the earth, stakes that are high enough to give one's life for. Already, she says, the rich are preparing to evacuate the earth and live in orbiting space stations that will drop down giant flexible tubes to pick up supplies of water and air. She ends by shouting, "This is war! We are not afraid to die to save the earth!" (728). The predictions of Green Vengeance are as bizarre as they appear to be in this summary, but in the overall story of the novel, they have their place, just as everything else does.

The Barefoot Hopi speaks next and draws upon his global travels to offer his listeners the kind of perspective that readers enjoy by seeing the plot lines converge. His speech is mesmerizing and pulls the cynical Angelita, Lecha, and Zeta into his spell. He begins by reading a message left by the eco-warriors who died in the destruction of the dam. It is full of happiness and praise to the earth, and they declare that in dying for the river, they have returned to "the source, the energy of the universe." The Barefoot Hopi offers his own explanation by stating that these brave souls are now "part of a single configuration of energy." The address then moves to a condemnation of the United States. The poisoning of the water, land, and air are acts of terrorism, unlike the actions of the eco-warriors, which are heroic. Politicians and bankers raid the U.S. Treasury while poor people begging for food are locked up. The spirits of the earth hate the destroyers, which is why the sun burns the cities and the water is drying up. Like Corn Woman, who retreats into the fourth world because of the neglect of her altar, the earth itself is withdrawing its gifts because of the abuses heaped upon it by the destroyers. The Hopi's vision of the future is apocalyptic and has the earth restoring the balance that has been thrown off in five hundred years of destruction. He concludes by referring to the other events that are happening worldwide and moving things in another direction:

> In Africa and in the Americas too, the giant snakes, Damballah and Quet-zalcoatl, have returned to the people. I have seen the snakes with my own eyes; they speak to the people of Africa, and they speak to the people of the Americas; they speak through dreams. The snakes say this: From out of the south the people are coming, like a great river flowing restless with the spirits of the dead who have been reborn again and again all over Africa and the Americas, reborn each generation more fierce and more numerous. Millions will move instinctively; unarmed and unguarded, they begin walking steadily north, following the twin brothers. (735)

The Hopi imagines a peaceful revolution where the reclamation of the land takes place without bloodshed. Angelita and Lecha, however, are not so idealistic. They know that great changes do not happen without violence, and they are eager for it. They smell blood. As Angelita says: "All hell was going to break loose. The best was yet to come" (749). Creative and destructive outlooks are so intertwined in the novel that it is hard to tell the difference at times. The threads of the stories wrap around each other to create a fabric of at least two colors. The Hopi's speech brings the two plot lines together in a creative way—the earth will reward the creators in its own terms. Angelita and Lecha, to name only two, weave the stories in a destructive way—the oppressors will be punished by their own devices and schemes, and the work of destruction needs assistance from the likes of Angelita and Lecha.

Silko brings the strands of the web to an apocalyptic end, or so we think. As the twins march north, the plot lines converge, and Angelita's prediction of all hell breaking loose begins to be fulfilled, we find Sterling in a car with Lecha and Seese. The car is careening out of the driveway of the Tucson ranch, and Lecha is driving over the dead guard dogs. The ranch has been invaded by Zeta's and Ferro's enemies, and Lecha has been dreaming of army helicopters carrying back the wounded from the war in Mexico.[7] They are headed for Wilson Weasel Tail's secret hideout in South Dakota where they will meet up with others in the armageddon of the Americas. Lecha has dreamed it all: natural disasters that will wipe out great chunks of the United States and its wealth, earthquakes in Japan, drought and heat that will send families north, even a European invasion by indigenous peoples from the south. Only Canada will remain an ally of the United States in the last great Indian war. The old almanac sums it up as "civil strife, civil crisis, civil war."

Just as the end approaches, the novel shifts to a final section titled simply "Home." Lecha, Seese, and Sterling are passing through Mesita, near Laguna, and Sterling asks to be let out. They all say good-bye, and Sterling begins to walk toward his home. He recognizes home in the taste of the water that is pumped from the windmill at the sheep camp, but he is also in shock from recent events and needs a few days to recover. When he awakes, he feels refreshed and has a new outlook on life. The popular magazines that served to orient him in the past are no longer meaningful in the present. He no longer diagnoses his emotional state according to tests taken in these magazines. In fact, he realizes that that world never really existed except in the glossy pages. Now he is ready to live out the prophecies and morality of his native heritage, and he does so by spending time with the earth. The sounds of civilization are far away as he sits beneath red sandstone cliffs and white clouds and begins to focus on his immediate surroundings: "He purposely kept his mind focused on the things he could see or touch; he avoided thinking about the day before or even the hour before, and he did not think about tomorrow" (757). Sterling is experiencing a different politics of time in a dimension with an eternal present. His experience is identical to Tayo's when he is on the mountain searching for the cattle. Time has not stopped; rather, he is experiencing story time, where all is present, and there are no boundaries. Like Tayo, he continues walking aimlessly until he finds himself at the uranium mine. For a while he walks through wild purple asters and thinks about the return of the buffalo to the Great Plains, but he has realized that there is a destination to his journey. He must visit the shrine of the sacred snake. He sees the uranium tailings first, and they prompt him to think of the people's opposition to the mine and the prophecies about the destruction that will follow. Before the end of the war, they had already seen the bright light of the first atomic explosion and the device that would later obliterate half a million Japanese. Now he has come full circle both geographically and spiritually, and the pattern begins to emerge.

As he approaches the shrine of the great stone snake, Sterling recalls its connections with Mexico. It was in Mexico, he remembers, that the original destroyers, the Gunadeeyahs, began. These Gunadeeyahs were sorcerers who had an appetite for blood that was combined with their sexual desires. Like many of the characters in the novel, they derived great sexual pleasure from the sight and taste of blood. Montezuma, according to the old stories, was the biggest sorcerer of all, and his advisors and descendants were the ones who caused the old ones to flee to the north: "They had been excited by the sacrifice victim's feeble struggle; they had lapped up the first rich spurts of hot blood. The Gunadeeyah clan had been born" (760). As these stories wrap themselves around Sterling's mind, he thinks to himself that the appearance of the Europeans was part of the old sorcery. As Yoeme had told Lecha and Zeta, the Spaniards were arriving with blood in their nostrils from the Inquisition and were ready for more. He thinks: "No wonder Cortes and Montezuma had hit it off together when they met; both had been members of the same secret clan" (760).

The uranium mine is the work of the same destroyers. Just as the theft of the stone idols was a part of the same story as the filming of the snake, the story of the Gunadeeyahs is present, not past. As Sterling sits near the snake, he reflects upon the twisted plots of his life and of those around him in Tucson and offers a summation for both himself and the reader:

> The snake didn't care if people were believers or not; the work of the spirits and prophecies went on regardless. Spirit beings might appear anywhere, even near open-pit mines. The snake didn't care about the uranium tailings; humans had desecrated only themselves with the mine, not the earth. Burned and radioactive, with all humans dead, the earth would still be sacred. Man was too insignificant to desecrate her.

Sterling understands the snake's message now, and the novel ends by noting that "the snake was looking south, in the direction from which the twin brothers and the people would come" (763).

From plots and subplots all around the world and from a variety of characters with a variety of agendas, the climax of the novel occurs with Sterling, the moral center, sitting alone beside the stone snake in the middle of tailings from an abandoned uranium mine. Here Silko puts a fine point on her implicit arguments about the political nature of time. As the Laguna delegation that went in search of the stone idols knew, the time would come for earth to balance things out. It may be five hundred years from now, but the time will come nonetheless. As nonnative readers wait for an apocalyptic "end," Silko provides a creative beginning, leaving the story open.

Technology

For Silko there are two ways of being in the world. In one humans are at odds with themselves, their creations, and their environment, separated by fragmenting and disorienting interpretations. In another, human beings are centered in a multiplying reflection of the cosmos whose focus is not the individual but the dynamic relationship of all things connected by stories. The former are the destroyers, and the latter are the creators. Both destroyers and creators use technology. For the destroyers, their tools exist outside themselves and are simply means to a particular disingenuous end. For the creators, technology is integrated into the very fabric of existence itself and serves to enhance and extend life. We saw these two ways of being in the world in *Ceremony*. In *Almanac* the destroyers have achieved frightening power.

In *Almanac of the Dead,* each understanding of technology mirrors the other as the plot, which is history itself, works its way to its semiapocalyptic end. This novel offers a kind of technological mimesis where ancient traditions of creation are mirrored in contemporary devices of destruction. Creators see these connections, but destroyers see only differences and have no connection to the past or future. A good example of the mirroring of the earth and technology occurs in the blood and electricity motifs. Images of blood dominate the novel and serve to depict the Native concept of networking, which is countered on the Euro-American side by electricity and, of course, computer networks. For Native people all over the world, the earth spirits communicate through the blood of their children. Damballah, Quetzalcoatl, and Spider Woman all speak to those who are connected by blood and stories and instruct them in the coming revolution. Those who do not get the message are technophiles of various kinds consumed by such things as gun-running, the sale of body parts taken from homeless people, torture videotapes, and an array of sexual experimentation.

The novel works to dissolve the differences wrought by Euro-American technology through a narration that encompasses both types of technology in a story about the end of white culture and the reconstitution of the earth and her native peoples. The mirroring of Native and Western uses and abuses of technology is especially telling in the setting of Tuxtla, Mexico. In Tuxtla Tacho is a native person who serves as a chauffeur for Menardo, an effete Mexican who has garnered his wealth by providing security services for the rich and powerful in Tuxtla (read CIA). Tacho is privy to special information through his ability to gamble and interpret Menardo's dreams, but in these interpretations he never gives Menardo the complete story. He cannot do so because Menardo is an assassination target of local Marxists who have placed Tacho there in order to gather intelligence on Menardo and his clients until the appropriate time for the assassination. Menardo, in the meantime, has become obsessed with security technology, in particular a bulletproof vest that one of his American Mafia clients has given to him. Ultimately, the vest becomes a fetish for him, and he prefers reading the technical information about the vest to being in the presence of his wife. Menardo eventually comes to wear the vest constantly, even during sex and sleep. Now thoroughly obsessed, Menardo devises a scheme to exhibit the power of his new fetish. He arranges to have Tacho fire a 9mm pistol at him just as his CIA friends arrive at the club. Menardo will pull off a marvelous practical joke, which is a notorious rite of passage for this group, and will also demonstrate how the man in charge of security is the most secure person in the elite group. As the men arrive, Menardo loudly commands Tacho to fire so that all may hear, and, of course, the vest fails. The assassination is effected by Menardo himself, and Tacho's innocence is guaranteed. Unlike the Mexican blankets that are woven so tight that water beads up on them in the rain, the bulletproof vest proves to be woven too loosely. This scene enacts a powerful ironic reversal of the massacre at Wounded Knee in 1890, where Ghost Dance shirts worn by the Lakota failed to protect them from the soldiers' bullets as they assumed. The technology of the destroyers becomes the tool of their own destruction as the witchery begins to implode. In *Almanac* Euro-American culture is unraveling thread by thread in both its spirituality and its technology. In Native cultures, on the other hand, technology is used both to thwart the otherness of Euro-American culture and to spin a web of stories that offers Native peoples all over the world a way to see how land, history, and technology all cohere into a reconstituted world where Native people take back their lands from Alaska to Chile.

An Alaskan medicine woman in *Almanac of the Dead* aptly represents how storytelling and technology weave a web that overcomes witchery and destruction. A satellite television is installed in her Yupik village, and most of the villagers ignore it or fall asleep in front of it. The woman has a pelt that is sacred to her and becomes the channel she uses to lock in on the spirits of the ancestors. The television enhances the power of the pelt by the appropriation of the satellite signals. Silko writes: "The old woman had gathered great surges of energy out of the atmosphere, by summoning spirit beings through the recitations of the stories that were also indictments of the greedy destroyers of the land. With the stories the old woman was able to assemble powerful forces flowing from the spirits of the ancestors" (156). The old Yupik woman uses her pelt, her stories, and a weather map on the television screen successfully to crash an airplane that is carrying surveyors and equipment from American oil companies. When the insurance adjuster arrives and someone suggests that the number of airplane crashes in the area could be explained by the same forces at work as in the Bermuda Triangle, he replies, "None of that stuff is true. It can all be explained" (160).

Indeed it can, and that is the problem of history and of the future as Silko paints them. Americans have been developing the capacity for explanation for so long that they have been hypnotized by their own accounts and measurements and can no longer see anything else. Explanation supplants meaning and creates a lack of vision, an inability to see larger relationships, the larger story. Blind and greedy officials lead blind and greedy citizens into the end of history in *Almanac of the Dead*. Meanwhile, Native people are reconstituting themselves through the ancient connection of blood and stories and are slowly but surely beginning the process of taking back the land.

Time

As mentioned earlier, the opening pages of *Almanac of the Dead* are not text but a map with Tucson at the center. Boxes of information on the map function as interpretive guides. In one of these boxes we read the following statement: "Sixty million Native Americans died between 1500 and 1600. The defiance and resistance to things European continue unabated. The Indian Wars have never ended in the Americas. Native Americans seek nothing less than the return of all tribal lands" (17). Leslie Marmon Silko is neither shy nor cryptic about the future or the past. She relentlessly details the diverse crimes, whether legal or cultural, committed against Native Americans and the Laguna Pueblo to this day. And she does so with the calm persistence of a person who knows her past and her future as well as her place and mission in the present. Native Americans will take back their lands; the process is already underway. That process is driven by storytelling, by replacing the stories of the invaders with a narrative that is both strong and fragile.

Almanac of the Dead ends on just this note. Sterling returns to his Laguna home where he walks out to the uranium mine and surveys the destruction. Silko writes: "Ahead all he could see were mounds of tailings thirty feet high, uranium waste blowing in the breeze, carried by the rain to springs and rivers. Here was the new work of the Destroyers; here was the destruction and poison. Here was where life ended" (760). Or where it would end if there were no creators in the world. In recent years a stone formation has emerged in the shape of the great snake. Only the traditionals can see this snake, and to most whites, such as the film crew, it is completely undetectable. But for Sterling it is a sign of life among the ruins of white culture. And although it remains invisible to that dominant culture, it nonetheless arises from the rubble, solid and secure. Further, the great stone snake points the way to the future, which is in the south and from which will come a horde of native people led by the heroic twins of myth and legend. The history of blood and earth is the history that will survive, whereas the destroyers are already passing away.

Almanac of the Dead works to show a deeper technology than that which continually enchants Western culture, especially in the late twentieth century. The earth has always been networked, Silko argues, through the energies of blood and spirits and human beings who seek not to destroy but to create. The witchery of the destroyers always turns upon itself while the creators wait patiently in the web of the earth. In fact, Silko herself is a creator since she employs the technology of writing and the publishing industry in order to disseminate the stories that will energize the reclamation of the land. What emerges from Silko's narration is that storytelling is not only a process of dissolving the rigid differences upon which Euro-American culture depends, it is also a process of decolonization. Precontact storytelling knit the tribe together under shifting conditions, and postcontact and contemporary stories function as a narrative web that holds destruction at bay. The spider is also known for her bite, and in *Almanac* she bites.

The accomplishments of *Almanac of the Dead* are bound to be explored more and more as readers and critics digest the novel. What we can say for sure is that it stands as one of the most striking critiques of Western culture, or death cultures in general, to date. The very structure of the novel leads us out of the parochialism of our limited worldviews and demands that we see a larger story, whether we like it or not. Unapologetic and unyielding in its indictment of the ideologies of destruction, the novel creates chaos and then offers a new creation myth from which a new world will emerge. As Janet St. Clair notes: "Like *Ceremony* and *Storyteller, Almanac of the Dead* is a story that rises above its own tangled plot lines to reveal both the confluence of seemingly fragmented stories and the order that such confluence implies. The myriad plots are finally understood not as lines at all, but as great looping convergences that encompass more time, and more space, until time and space—those cornerstones of modern Western thought—become the eviscerated signifiers of a radically limited vision. . . . The almanac, timeless chronicle of recurring histories, becomes a symbol of hope and continuance" (St. Clair, 87–88).

Such a view is not unique to Silko and can be found in other writings by Native Americans. For example, consider the following remarks by Vine Deloria Jr.: "It would be impossible for the thoughtless or impious acts of one species to have an immediate drastic [effect] on the earth. The cumulative effect of continuous secularity, however, poses a different kind of danger. Long-standing prophecies tell us of the impious people who would come here, defy the creator, and cause massive destruction of the planet. . . . The cumulative evidence of global warming, acid rain, the disappearance of amphibians, overpopulation, and other products of civilized life certainly testify to the possibility of these prophecies being correct."[8] Even nonnative writers, like certain Euro-Americans in the novel, sense that destruction is a distinct possibility and narrate that sense of dread into apocalyptic literature.[9] What Silko has done in

Almanac of the Dead is give voice to those ideas that Deloria and others detail in prose. She does more than that, however, for she provides a hope that other writers do not. Out of the chaos of *Almanac,* possibilities emerge like land in a creation story. The hope lies in the land, the only thing that lasts from life to life, and the land has the last word because it has a time all its own.

Chapter Seven

Yellow Woman and a Beauty
of the Spirit: Notes and Essays

Leslie Marmon Silko is known primarily as a novelist, secondarily as a
writer of short fiction, and less so as a poet. We have seen that her talents as a writer are not limited to particular genres, and her poetry and
short stories are as profound as her novels. With *Yellow Woman and a
Beauty of the Spirit: Essays on Native American Life Today,* Silko's nonfiction
prose is made available to a wider audience.[1] A collection of essays she
wrote between 1984 and 1996, this book includes addresses ("Language
and Literature from a Pueblo Indian Perspective"), forewords to other
books ("The Indian with a Camera"), and author's notes from some of
her own books ("As a Child I Loved to Draw and Cut Paper"). Although
there are a number of pieces in the collection, 22 in all, Silko makes it
clear that the essay is a form she is somewhat uncomfortable with and
ambivalent about in spite of the fact that during the editing of this book
she was also hard at work on an essay on rocks. She notes that "as I
toiled over bland prose and argued with magazine editors, I would
regret that I had ever agreed to write nonfiction, and I would swear off
nonfiction prose forever" (14). She writes that "secretly I hoped that the
struggle with these other pieces of nonfiction would empower me to
bring forth my essays on rain and on rocks" (14). The essay on rain was
published in 1993 as *Sacred Water.* An early version of the essay on rocks
appears in this volume.

Silko describes the structure of the book as "like a spider's web" and
suggests that we see the book beginning with the land, which is also the
center of the web. Radiating from this center are strands that concern
human identity, imagination, and storytelling, and these strands take
the form of essays with topics from national policy to hunger. The next
section of essays deals with the "representation and visualization of narrative, of storytelling," and in this section Silko shares some of her
research into Mayan and Aztec screenfold books as well as her thoughts
about the visual medium in general. The final section of essays is her
favorite because it includes an excerpt of "An Essay on Rocks." This section

119

also includes essays on photography and nonfiction prose. Because the demarcations between the sections that Silko mentions in her introduction are not obvious, the book can be divided along the lines she mentions but with some flexibility regarding which essay belongs in which section.

The Land

The first three essays of *Yellow Woman and a Beauty of the Spirit* are explicitly concerned with the land. The longest essay in the book is also the first and is titled "Interior and Exterior Landscapes: The Pueblo Migration Stories." It explores in six sections some of the foundational concepts in Pueblo mythology and worldview. In fact, the six sections of this essay, first published in 1986, adumbrate the style of *Almanac of the Dead,* where the model is Mayan and Aztec books. The six sections are diverse and concern topics such as the aridity of the New Mexico plateaus and the idea of landscape as a character in fiction, but the web is clearly there being spun in fine fashion. "Interior and Exterior Landscapes," because of its carefully crafted structure and elegant articulation of important insights into Pueblo history, myth, and worldview is the best essay in the collection. Readers should look here to find a thorough articulation of the ideas that inform Silko's writing.

The first section of the essay is titled "From a High Arid Plateau in New Mexico" and discusses Pueblo burial customs. The ancient Pueblos[2] buried their dead in vacant or crumbling rooms off the main living areas where they also threw debris and other cast-off items. Contrary to some anthropological speculations, these human remains were not considered garbage; rather, they were simply in an appropriate resting place in their journey back to dust. The items in the rooms were equally valued and understood as being on a journey during which their decomposition would benefit living members of the earth until they disappeared completely. This view, common in Native American cultures, is difficult to understand for contemporary Euro-Americans for whom excess is understood much differently.[3]

In the second section of the essay, "From the Emergence Place," Silko discusses the notion of landscape for the Pueblos. She begins by noting that the term *landscape,* when defined as that which is limited to the eye's purview, is an inadequate description of the Pueblos' relationship to the earth because it assumes that the viewer is privileged. In Pueblo understanding, it is the landscape itself that is privileged, and the viewer cannot be seen as outside or separate from what is seen and not seen by the eye. Extrapolating from this observation, Silko makes an interesting point about representation in art: Realism, as understood in painting and sculpture, is a concept alien to the Pueblo worldview. The reason is that for ancient and traditional Pueblos, nothing exists in isolation, everything is connected. Another way of saying this is that the Pueblos are anti-Platonic; there is no perfect form of a boulder or a deer; rather, there is only the boulder or deer in a complex and fragile relationship to its surroundings, which would include history and story as well as material objects. Pueblos are not interested in the one, nor are they interested solely in the many. What they are interested in is relation. As we saw in Silko's fiction and poetry, it is the relationships that matter, not the elements themselves. Tayo is healed when he finally sees the pattern, Andy is initiated as he learns about the value of not finding the thing you are looking for, and the Yupik woman in *Almanac* is able to master contemporary technology by understanding relationships. This understanding means that "a lifelike rendering of an elk is too restrictive" because "only the elk *is* itself," not the drawing. Representation in the Pueblo worldview concerns itself with relationships rather than isolated elements. This point cannot be overemphasized. Silko, in continuing the oral tradition of the ancient Pueblos, is continuing the valuation of relationships, and these relationships are not hierarchical but dialogical and context-specific. These associations, moreover, are deeply complex and easily broken. The story of the Gambler that appears in *Storyteller* offers a good example of the importance of connections between all things and the imbalance that results when the harmony is upset. We recall that the Gambler, in his desire to have bigger stakes with which to wager, stole the rain clouds and kept them in one of his rooms. His greed, or we might say, his denial of relation, caused the entire earth to suffer.

In the next section, "Through the Stories We Hear Who We Are," Silko discusses the remarkable ability of her people to survive and even thrive in the harsh climate of the arid Southwest. She suggests that in such a culture information is vital (the location of springs, the forecasting of weather, orientation), and the best way to convey information in an oral culture is through story. The oral tradition reflects the collective memory of the people and provides for the transmission of that memory through succeeding generations. When the only means of maintaining and transmitting information is narrative, the stories take on a depth dimension that is hard to imagine for those who live in a culture of books and bytes. Silko suggests that the wide net cast by the stories to

include everything worth remembering is directly related to the remarkable inclusivity characteristic of Native American tribes in general. As
Silko notes, "Everything became a story" (31). Not only did everything
become a story, stories themselves became remarkably flexible, able to
absorb new knowledge while allowing irrelevant information to drop
out. This phenomenon produced an approach to language and interpretation that Western culture is only now beginning to glimpse: "The
ancient Pueblo people sought a communal truth, not an absolute truth.
For them this truth lived somewhere within the web of differing versions, disputes over minor points, and outright contradictions tangling
with old feuds and village rivalries" (32). The truth as in-between is
inherent in Native American comprehension of the world. This aspect of
their worldview made it especially difficult for them initially to choose
between Christianity and their own traditions; they saw no reason why
they could not live in the spaces between.

The stories spin themselves around particular elements of the landscape, and Silko notes that it is impossible to tell which came first, the
story or the landscape to which the story refers. For example, she recalls
a boulder on the road to Paguate that is supposedly the heart of a monster who was threatening Kochininako before the twins killed him and
tossed his heart as far as they could. She notes that there are plenty of
boulders around the area, but only one is the heart of a monster. The
stories cannot be separated from the land, and the land cannot be interpreted without a story. These ideas are the subject of the next section of
the essay about the migration story. For Silko and the traditional Pueblos, the migration stories that detail the travels of the Laguna to their
appropriate place after emergence are stories about interior landscapes
as well. "The Emergence," Silko notes, "was an emergence into a precise
cultural identity" (36). She also states that the journeys involved in the
emergence and migration were journeys of "awareness and imagination"
involving understanding the difference between being in the earth and
being outside the earth." The difference is important, for after emergence one becomes aware of relation, the difference in exterior surroundings that produce a difference in identity. This notion is under-
scored by the fact that it is only with the help of badger and antelope
that the people emerge at all, and without that interdependence there
is no identity. Silko points out that the ability to imagine this interdependence enables them to emerge culturally: "Only at the moment
that the requisite balance between human and *other* was realized could the
Pueblo people become a culture, a distinct group whose population and

survival remained stable despite the vicissitudes of the climate and terrain" (38).

She also notes the similarity between landscape and dreams. Both, she asserts, have the ability to produce strong emotional responses that can be channeled into ritual and narrative forms. This translation of the dramatic experience of landscape and dream serves a double function: It contextualizes the experience for the individual and strengthens the group's values relative to such experiences. The individual exists between extinction and survival, and the only thing that keeps the individual on one side or the other is the fragile and delicate web of ritual and narrative. This observation is especially true in the Southwest, where everything is an ally in the struggle for survival. The vast distances ironically compress the earth and sky so that one feels as if there is not much space between one and the elements of the earth and sky: "One look and you know that simply to survive is a great triumph, that every possible resource is needed, every possible ally—even the most humble insect or reptile" (41). Silko recalls feeling the web of the story surround her as she listened to her Aunt Susie tell an ancient story about a location in which she had wandered. Her intimate familiarity with the landscape of the story allowed her to merge with the story's language so that a particular "place" was created that resonates with meaning. The essay ends with a discussion of the landscape as a character in fiction, especially Silko's own "Storyteller." "Interior and Exterior Landscapes" is a marvelous tale about the stories that matter most to Silko. In this essay we find a succinct and profound articulation of the ideas that empower and shape Silko's writing.

In "Language and Literature from a Pueblo Indian Perspective," Silko rehearses some of the ideas in the previous essay. This essay is the text of a speech given at the English Institute. A critical contribution of the essay is the short phrase "language is story" (50). Silko believes that this is one of the more important contributions of Native American cultures to the English language. The idea that each word has a story itself and that storytelling, by using words, is the structuring of multiple stories anticipates much of contemporary literary theory, especially that of Mikhail Bakhtin, Jacques Derrida, and Michel Foucault. At the same time, the Native American understanding of language is unique in its emphasis upon narrative as the root of all words and in the ubiquitous function of narrative. Whereas contemporary literary theorists such as Paul Ricoeur and Roland Barthes have called for the exploration of a sentential linguistics, that is, a linguistics based on the sentence rather than the word, Native Americans have been operating with a functional narrative linguistics that finds the heart of meaning in narratives rather than words or sentences.

"Yellow Woman and a Beauty of the Spirit" is a rumination upon landscape and beauty in the Pueblo imagination. In this essay Silko retells some of the most important stories from her childhood in order to examine the notion of beauty in the landscape and people. This notion of beauty is drawn from the idea of balance rather than the sense of something exceptional, as it is in Western culture. Again the fundamental idea is the importance of relation; therefore, beauty is that which evidences relation, and the archetypal figure here is Yellow Woman, who is willing to risk all to explore relationships. There are implications for ethics in the idea of beauty found at Laguna, and one of these is the lack of absolutes whether in regard to truth, beauty, or goodness: "In this universe, there is no absolute good or absolute bad; there are only balances and harmonies that ebb and flow. Some years the desert receives abundant rain, other years there is too little rain, and sometimes there is so much rain that floods cause destruction. But rain itself is neither innocent or guilty. The rain is simply itself" (64). Thus beauty is harmony and balance, and it is Kochininako, Yellow Woman, who typifies such balance by having the courage to act sensually, rather than violently or destructively.

Identity, Imagination, and Storytelling

As the essays move into the topics of this section, they employ a tone that is at times more distant and also more political. For example, the next essay, "America's Debt to the Indian Nations," is an excursus on a Commission on Civil Rights Publication titled "Indian Tribes: A Continuing Quest for Survival" and is written in a style that is more academic than the previous essays. This essay is a good example of Silko's continuing interest in legal matters and legal discourse. Following upon this essay, however, is one in which Silko returns to the personal. Having been asked by *Mother Jones* magazine in 1984 to imagine what another four years with Ronald Reagan as president would mean for Native Americans, Silko turns to her Auntie Kie for an interview. This is a person who does not appear in her other stories, but she is quite a character nonetheless. In this essay Silko defers to Auntie Kie, who rails about U.S. policy and practice toward Native Americans over the last 400 years. In fact, one of the interesting subplots of this short essay is how

Auntie Kie continually cuts Silko off as she tries in vain to direct the conversation: "But as I begin to open my mouth, she sees, and before I can take a breath she is right on me" (82). Auntie Kie is intelligent, articulate, factual, and fiery in her diatribe on American policy, which includes references to international money policy, the relative powers of the Supreme Court and Congress, the important 1832 decision by Justice John Marshall about Indian sovereignty and President Andrew Jackson's cynical and sinister response, and the general function of the president in American culture. Of the latter she notes that "American presidents are just there to give the people a good show." This essay depicts Silko as interviewer and author, an engaging combination that does not appear anywhere else in her work.

The remaining essays in this section deal with similar themes. In "The People and the Land ARE Inseparable," Silko recounts the development of her own understanding of the land, from the confusion she first experienced in trying to grasp the exact boundary used by white culture to the respect for the land that she learned from her ancestors, family, and friends. She shifts back to an academic voice edged with political criticism for "Tribal Councils: Puppets of the U.S. Government." Here she explains the reason that some tribes have deforested their wilderness, allowed strip mining, clear-cutting, and disposing of radioactive waste on their lands. The reason is, of course, that these things are done not by traditionals on the reservation but by government-sanctioned tribal councils. The corruption of these councils is notorious since they were established by the Indian Reorganization Act of 1941. Continuing in the vein of political criticism, Silko next includes the essay "Hunger Stalked the Tribal People." This is a unique articulation of the role of hunger in the colonial enterprise, a factor that is often underestimated in other accounts of the decimation of tribal cultures. She contrasts the colonial use of hunger as a tool of oppression and greed with the Pueblo responses to hunger. An important story in the essay concerns the difficulties the Navajo had adapting to the region. Because their harvests were often poor, the Navajo took to raiding Pueblo storehouses and stock. Grandmother Anaya remembers an incident, recalled in *Storyteller,* concerning a group of Navajo men who stole some Pueblo sheep but were caught fairly quickly by her grandfather. When asked why they resorted to stealing, the Navajos replied that their people were starving and there was nothing else to do but steal. The Laguna men gave the Navajos some of the sheep and told them to come and ask, and they would be given food. This incident inaugurates the summer and fall feasts when Navajos, Apaches, and other people outside the pueblos are refused nothing when they ask. Silko does not romanticize this incident; on the contrary, she suggests that it is common sense. The same sort of common sense is found in the origin of Thanksgiving, when Indians "realized that hungry pilgrims, like all hungry human beings, might be dangerous." She goes on to write: "It isn't great spirituality or generosity but simple human intelligence that says that when some are well fed and some are hungry, the hungry people must be fed; otherwise there can be no peace or security for those with food" (98). This statement, we may recall, is reflected in the Stone Avenue Mural, where the message is about the revolution that will occur because of the people's hunger.

The final two essays in this section are personal accounts of stops by the border patrol. Like the other items in the section, they reflect on identity, especially in the way that borders affect identity for those who guard them as well as those who would cross them. Both essays describe terrifying and angry altercations with the border patrol. Typically, Silko finds an ally in the German shepherd who is there to sniff for drugs: "The dog had an innate dignity, an integrity that did not permit her to serve those men" (110). The scene, while horrific, is also instructive. In the midst of intense harassment by agents assigned to prevent crossing an imaginary line, Silko develops a relationship across a more obvious border and communes with an animal. This "true story" has all the elements of a *hummah-hah* story from the past, where conversation with the animals could aid in one's survival. The story is not mere affectation but provides, Silko believes, for her and her companion's survival that night on a lonely stretch of highway in the New Mexico desert.

The Representation of Storytelling

Ma ah shra true ee, the Giant Serpent, is the incarnation of a story. He appeared in the spring of 1980 at the Jackpile uranium mine in the village of Paguate. The Giant Serpent surfaced as a "biomorphic configuration" of yellow sandstone and darker ores at the base of the huge piles of uranium tailings. The serpent is said to be a messenger from the fourth world, where he has stayed since the people broke open the lake where he lived because of jealousy. The message of the snake is unclear, but Silko sees a connection between its appearance and the recent history of the uranium mine. Since the mine began blasting open the earth near the *sipapu,* or emergence place, Laguna and its seven villages have suffered terrible tragedies, from teenage suicide pacts to motiveless murders. The traditionals do not see these events as acts of an angry god toward the sinners he holds in his hand; rather, they interpret these events as effects with a particular cause. Violating the earth with such greedy and imbalanced intentions is bound to result in disastrous consequences, as the history of our use of nuclear products confirms. The appearance of Ma ah shra true ee signals the disappearance of Euro-American ways but not the Euro-Americans themselves. As a visual representation of a story, the Giant Serpent produces more stories that function as interpretations.

Other essays in this section relate Silko's experiences of researching the novel *Almanac of the Dead,* where the Giant Serpent plays an important role, and her efforts to complete the novel on Stone Avenue in Tucson. She includes a photograph of her mural of the giant snake. The snake is still there at 930 North Stone Avenue in Tucson. I stood before it, walked up and down the length of it, and saw the pastel colors coming off on my fingertips as I touched it. As I looked more closely, I saw some faint writing as well. Scratched on the mural with a kind of pen were phrases such as "Yes!," "Thank You. We love you," and "Irish liberation." These words were written directly under Silko's word *Revolución.* Like Ma ah shra true ee in Laguna, Silko has created an icon that draws people and their stories to it.

Rocks, Writing, and Photography

The final section of *Yellow Woman and a Beauty of the Spirit* contains new and old essays, from her essay on rocks to the autobiographical notes to *Laguna Woman* and *Sacred Water.* The section begins with the author's note to *Sacred Water,* where Silko describes her need to deal with books in a hands-on fashion. Here is the story of her first publication in the fifth grade as well as the rationale behind the publication of *Sacred Water.* "The Indian with a Camera" and "On Photography" are fascinating pieces that articulate Silko's philosophy of the photographic image as well as its role in storytelling and political discourse. Tracing the Pueblo interest in the image as a viable medium for storytelling to ancient petroglyphs and kiva art, Silko discusses the camera as yet another way for Native Americans to tell a story with an image. She recalls her own family ceremonies of storytelling precipitated by the viewing of photographs in a tall Hopi basket. Pueblo history includes an openness to the white man's camera that lasted until it became clear that it was being used in voyeuristic fashion in sacred ceremonies or for the political end of prosecuting caciques who were illegally practicing the Pueblo religion instead of Christianity. Always aware of the intimate nature of the photographic image, the Pueblo people were forced to limit access, photographic and otherwise, to their private lives and rituals. Now that eye is beginning to turn back upon Euro-American culture as it records not only the devastation wrought by colonialism but also the existence of Native Americans and their defiance in the face of those abuses. Silko writes: "The Indian with a camera is an omen of a time in the future that all Euro-Americans unconsciously dread: the time when the indigenous people of the Americas will retake their land. Euro-Americans distract themselves with whether a real, or traditional, or authentic Indian would, should, or could work with a camera" (178). That the camera should be an important element in the reclamation of the land should not be a surprise to those who read *Almanac of the Dead,* where the technology of the decadent implodes and the oppressed use it in their own liberation.

"An Essay on Rocks" is an excerpt of a longer essay that combines images and words to explore a prominent feature of the landscape in the American Southwest. In this excerpt the reader follows Silko on a walk around her home in the Saguaro National Monument just northwest of Tucson. The dark lava and ash are the result of a huge volcanic explosion long ago, so huge that it destroyed the volcano itself and left only the lava and strange rock formations. The story begins with Silko on a ridge looking down an arroyo containing a black shape against the white sand. Silko interprets this image as something unusual—a blackened carcass, a floor safe, the head of a horse, a steamer trunk. As we follow her down the ridge to examine the enigmatic shape, we are treated to a photograph of the terrain and a story about the hills outside of Tucson. We learn that these hills have a history more recent than the volcanic one; this has been the refuge of criminals of one kind or another. Out here is loot from a 1917 train robbery, bootleggers with their stills, duffel bags full of cash and cocaine that have been dumped from airplanes in the middle of the night, and victims of heinous acts whose bodies are buried in shallow graves and covered with spider webs and weeds. As she approaches the form in the arroyo, her hands are wet with anticipation, and we see a photograph of what she sees: a black form in the middle of the wash. It could be any of the things she has mentioned or something else altogether. As we turn the page we again see what she sees, that it is "only a black rock the size of an auto engine." "Those who pay no attention to rocks," she writes, "may be surprised, but the appearance of a rock may change from hour to hour" (191). She ends the essay by recalling the tale in *Storyteller* where she thinks she sees a bear, but it may be just a rock. This is a story about the joy and excitement of interpretation, and it is one that is well suited to the Southwest, where images appear and shift with each interpretation. This essay resonates with me in a special way. While hiking on top of the mesa overlooking the 640 acres of Marmon land near Acoma, I came around a huge boulder to see a bear outlined perfectly against a rock about 25 yards away. The hair on the back of my neck stood up, and I froze. When neither I nor the bear moved for several minutes, I realized that perhaps I was misinterpreting the image. As I slowly moved closer, I could see that this was not a bear but an incredibly lifelike formation on the rock that was a much darker color than the sandstone around it. This phenomenon occurs often when hiking in the Southwest because the landscape itself generates a variety of interpretations, just as Silko describes in this book.

Yellow Woman and A Beauty of the Spirit offers readers yet another set of stories with which to imagine the world. Though the form is nonfiction prose, the stories are there nonetheless, as are images conjured up by the stories or Silko's camera. This collection of essays serves as an important source of information for the stories behind the other stories. They also show that Silko can speak in a discourse that is available to academics and others who want the "true stories" that the essay form provides. In this form as well, Silko is a fine storyteller.

Chapter Eight
Leslie Marmon Silko:
American Writer

Looking at Leslie Marmon Silko in the larger contexts of American and Native American literature, we find that, once again, she does not fit easily or completely into either category while her work enriches both. Categories do not worry her very much at all; she gives prominence to the story, and the story goes where it will regardless of the boundaries that we set for it. Such a perspective on narrative springs, like everything else, from her Laguna heritage where the world is made of stories, not categories. Her viewpoint on stories is especially intriguing, combining as it does a remarkable openness with a distinctly ethnic perspective. Therein lies the ingenuity of Silko's work and the genius of the culture that produced her. Ethnic particulars offer universal perspectives in Silko's worldview, and a celebration of tribal stories creates a remarkable receptivity to hearing other stories. Indeed, such openness has been dangerous for Native Americans since it exposed many sacred traditions to abuse by whites out for exotica or profit or both. Silko, however, believes what she says about stories and therefore knows that they have a power that will overcome and outlast anyone who would misuse them.

Her stories are nourished not only by her Laguna heritage but also by a hungry mind. Her reading includes Wittgenstein, Hume, Faulkner, Shakespeare, Milton, and Flannery O'Connor, to name a few. Per Seyersted tells the story of her visit to Norway when she discovered figures on the iron plates in his fireplace. "Oh there you have the three goats from that Norwegian fairy tale," she said.[1] She is remarkable in her ability to appreciate other stories and sift through them to determine their sources in creative or destructive forces. *Almanac of the Dead* is a good example of her ability to research, contextualize, and evaluate stories from all over the world.

When asked about her view of Native American aesthetics, she always answers consistently: "You can go and impose those differences, but I think that really strong writing springs from such depth of the psyche that there aren't such differences. You might be able to say that

all writing from those considered Other by the powers of life and death
has some similarities. But that includes gay people, immigrants, people
who have maybe been insane. . . . But to say, 'This is how Native American writing is different from African American,' I don't think so" (Perry,
334). From a much earlier interview, she notes: "Those definitions are
okay, if you have to begin to break things up into groups. . . . If everyone wants to talk about the same thing, it's useful to say that this will
be the group that's to talk about Ezra Pound, but I think that what
writers, storytellers, and poets have to say necessarily goes beyond such
trivial boundaries as origin. There's also the danger of demeaning literature when you label certain books by saying this is black, this is Native
American, and then, this is just writing. That's what's going on now,
and I don't like it" (Fisher, 21). Silko is a Native American writer who
does not believe in an exclusive Native American aesthetics. Nonnative
people can learn to appreciate Laguna stories as long as they make an
effort to understand the land that lies behind all the stories. Any narrative drawn from land and life has the potential to do what hers do; it
does not have to be traced to a Native American source. For example,
she encourages her students to read Flannery O'Connor: "I tell my students, 'Look, look what she's done.' The students'd say, 'Oh, she just
writes about the same old area and countryside.' 'Well,' I said, . . . 'that
in a sense is one of her greatest achievements, just to take these same
sorts of things again and again and again to make these magnificent stories, you know' " (Seyersted, 22). As long as the land is telling the story,
it is a story worth hearing in Silko's view.

It would be wrong to paint Silko as a writer who is attempting to
throw off all boundaries and simply ignore limitations in order to break
free of them. She knows that boundaries are real, as real as the relation
that is created by crossing them and as real as the danger involved in the
transgression. The limits concerning what is appropriate to reveal are
always being negotiated in the Native American writing community,
and often there are strenuous disagreements. Although she is respected
and even revered by other Native American writers in general, her relationships within that community have sometimes been strained. For
example, Paula Gunn Allen, a fellow Laguna writer and critic, takes
Silko to task for revealing a clan story in *Ceremony.* "She must have been
told, as I was, that we don't tell these things outside," Allen writes.[2]
Janet St. Clair points out that Allen herself violated this rule when she
compiled her own book, *Grandmothers of the Light,* under the instructions
of her spirit guides, who told her that she was permitted to reveal these

stories now because the time is right (St. Clair, 84). It is difficult not to see this conflict as the implicit conflict between Betonie and Ku'oosh in *Ceremony*. One writer sees the need for change whereas the other resists it, but ultimately all have to negotiate it. No other Native American writer is as clear about the fact that the problems in the world do not derive from ethnicity but from motivation. Any ethnocentrism at work in *Almanac of the Dead* is in the service of a larger story that offers hope to anyone willing to love and respect the earth.

Another example of these difficult negotiations of appropriate artistic expression finds Silko on the offensive. In her review of Louise Erdrich's *Beet Queen*, Silko castigates Erdrich for her acquiescence to postmodern influences, specifically, to self-referential writing. If we accept Silko's definition of "post-modern, self-referential writing," then it is easy to see why she objects to it: "Self-referential writing is light-years away from shared or communal experience that underlies oral narrative and modern fiction."[3] Silko's criticisms are head-on: Erdrich has forgotten about the land. Her characters are disconnected from the land on which they walk and from which they emerge. Instead, they reflect only language and the unconscious, conveniently forgetting about the history of blood, racism, and identity in South Dakota. Regardless of what we think about the fairness of Silko's criticism of Erdrich, it is easy to see where her loyalties lie. The land has a history, and that history must be part of the story.

As we think about Silko's place in the literary landscape, we must think of two worlds, the world of American literature in all of its manifestations and the world of Laguna with its local tales of mythic proportions. There are many bridges between these worlds, but three in particular stand out as Silko's contributions to the literary landscapes of American and Native American literature. These are land, language, and identity.

Land is one of the obsessions bequeathed to us as Americans, and this is in no small part due to the inherited guilt whites feel for dispossessing indigenous peoples from their land. The land on which the first Europeans landed was seen through the lenses of the Genesis myth. Paradise was regained, and the edict to "subdue the earth" was heartily followed by the visitors. The problem was that, for most of those colonizers, indigenous people were part of the earth that was to be subdued. The dominant culture in the United States still views land as something to be used until it is used up. Native American literature offers an implicit critique of American mythologies of the land that we all share, at least in principle. More than any other writer, Silko gives the earth a voice by making her the heroine of nearly every story. Whether she is speaking through women, men, or animals, the earth is embodied in these voices and calls us back to the very ground on which we stand. Silko accomplishes this not through metanarratives about the earth but through localized narratives with mythic content. The chronicle of American literature can be read as a history of the imagination of landscape. Whether it is Faulkner's Mississippi or Thoreau's Walden Pond or Whitman's open road, the land has always been at the center of the American literary imagination. With Leslie Marmon Silko's work comes a new chapter in the imagination of land in American literature. No writer has given the land such prominence and voice. The land envelops and sustains us and thereby conceals our differences and sustains our similarities. She is both source and destination for all of us, regardless of ethnicity. All these ideas flow out of Silko's writing.

While the land is a heroine for Silko, it is also a source of alienation. Being separated from the land is to be lost in a wilderness of broken histories and ideas. Its essential qualities make our inattention that much more dangerous. Without a center, we turn upon each other and the earth herself by substituting destructive manipulation for creative integration. It is a long fall from the land to ourselves. Left to ourselves we become nightmarish in our actions and agendas. We need a larger circle, a magic circle drawn around us that will not only protect us from the outside but also from ourselves. That ring is the earth and within her our differences are dampened in favor of our larger similarity as her children. These are the sacraments that Silko offers in her writing. Something is left that is holy in America, and we are standing upon it.

"When language touches land, place is created," notes Susan Scarberry.[4] It is impossible to imagine Silko's contributions to American letters without recognizing what she is able to do with language. Silko proclaims narrative as the beginning and end of all discourse. While theorists focus upon signifiers and signifieds, Silko tells stories that are heard across cultural divides that seem in other ways of communicating to be impassable. She does this by allowing language to live its own life, to tell the story of the earth in cadences and meters drawn from nature's rhythms. "Language is story," she tells us, and in so doing she sums up what philosophers of language have been aiming at for years. Language as story means that every word must be explained with a story of its own and met with patience and love. Language shapes time and space and caresses the earth. Language touching land creates place.

The story of America is the story of identity forged in the furnaces of land and language. Silko has an ability to blend land and language in ways that no other writer can to produce a unique identity for her characters and, by implication, for us. Through very private stories told within her family she can derive a significance that opens up to people far removed from her in time and space. Her characters willingly and unwillingly transgress all sorts of boundaries to produce an identity that is relative rather than individual. Indeed, this is another reason that Silko attacks Erdrich's fiction: She sees it as sacrificing the communal for the individual. For Silko identity is about relation. Yellow Woman is a prime example of this notion. She is willing to risk her life for relation and crosses the boundaries of river, time, and culture in order to experience it. That experience brings the gifts of broader vision in the form of stories to her people. In Silko's short story "Yellow Woman," the main character is uncertain about who she is once she crosses the boundaries of her familiar world. It is upon her return, after relation has been established, that she understands not only who she is but what her role in society is. She is there to blur the boundaries and promote relation. Likewise, when the Pueblo people emerged, it was into a "precise cultural identity" formed by the need to see themselves in relation to the elements of the fifth world. We see the result of maintaining rigid boundaries for the denial of relation in the acts and beliefs of the destroyers who seek nothing but death. Death is stasis, the absence of change. To be alive means to grow, Betonie tells us. Though "the people mistrust this greatly," to resist change is to die. Here Silko offers a much-needed if little-understood criticism of American ideas of individualism, rugged and otherwise. For her, identity comes through relation, transgression, and exploration. The self that emerges from these border crossings is not an isolated free agent but a whole person who recognizes his or her entanglement in all things. He or she is trapped in mother spider's web but can also see the pattern. As such the individual gains meaning by recognizing the pattern and valuing similarities over differences. To do otherwise is to cut ourselves off from the relations that define us. Silko is relentless in her acclamation of the need for relation and offers her readers ways to achieve it through narrative.

Leslie Marmon Silko is unique in her ability to combine such profound views of land, language, and identity into every one of her stories, whether it is a poem, an essay, or a novel. She calls us back to the land so that we may hear a familiar voice, one that speaks in a feminine language. Once we are reconnected to mother earth, we find our identity in relation with her and all her inhabitants. Then we know that this web of land, language, and identity is both fragile and strong. What remains is to continue spinning the web so that the story never ends. That is Silko's finest gift to the earth.

Notes and References

Chapter One

1. Lawrence J. Evers and Dennis W. Carr, "A Conversation with Leslie Marmon Silko," *Sun Tracks: An American Indian Literary Magazine* 3 (1976): 30.

2. Kim Barnes, "A Leslie Marmon Silko Interview," *Leslie Marmon Silko, "Yellow Woman,"* ed. Melody Graulich. *Women Writers: Texts and Contexts* (New Brunswick, N.J.: Rutgers University Press, 1993), 49–50; hereafter cited in text as Barnes.

3. Leslie Marmon Silko, "Contributors' Biographical Notes," *Voices of the Rainbow: Contemporary Poetry by American Indians,* ed. Kenneth Rosen (New York: Seaver, 1975), 230.

4. Leslie Marmon Silko, *Laguna Woman: Poems by Leslie Silko* (Greenfield Center, N.Y.: Greenfield Review Press, 1974), 41; hereafter cited in text as *LW*, or parenthetically in chapter 2.

5. Leslie Marmon Silko, *Yellow Woman and a Beauty of the Spirit: Essays on Native American Life Today* (New York: Simon & Schuster, 1996), 63; hereafter cited in text as *YWBS*, or parenthetically in chapter 7.

6. Leslie Marmon Silko, *Sacred Water: Narratives and Pictures* (Tucson, Ariz.: Flood Plain Press, 1993), 81; hereafter cited in text as *SW*, or parenthetically in chapter 5.

7. Leslie Marmon Silko, *Storyteller* (New York: Viking, 1981), 17–18; hereafter cited in text as *Storyteller*, or parenthetically in chapter 4.

8. Dexter Fisher, "Stories and Their Tellers: A Conversation with Leslie Marmon Silko," *The Third Woman: Minority Women Writers of the United States,* ed. Dexter Fisher (Boston: Houghton Mifflin Co., 1980), 23; hereafter cited in text as Fisher.

9. Per Seyersted, "Two Interviews with Leslie Marmon Silko," *American Studies in Scandinavia* 13 (1981): 24; hereafter cited in text as Seyersted.

10. AIM is a movement that began in the 1960s as a return to traditional tribal ways but increasingly has taken on political qualities largely because the American government has interpreted its traditionalism as revolutionary and dangerous. For a good history of Native American activism and AIM's role, see Vine Deloria Jr.'s *God is Red: A Native View of Religion* (Boulder, Colo.: Fulcrum, 1994).

11. Most of the uranium mined in the United States is done on Native American lands. Tailings are waste products produced by the mining process.

12. Governor Evan Mecham was responsible for Arizona's refusal to recognize Martin Luther King's Birthday as an official holiday. Artists, politicians, and others threatened to boycott or move to another state until Mecham was recalled.

135

Chapter Two

1.   This collection was later republished as George W. Cronyn, ed., *American Indian Poetry: An Anthology of Songs and Chants* (New York: Liveright, 1970).

2.   The Imagists employed free verse and were concerned with creating clear and precise images in their writing.

3.   Paula Gunn Allen, ed., *Studies in American Indian Literature: Critical Essays and Course Designs* (New York: MLA, 1983), xi.

4.   Duane Niatum, ed., *Harper's Anthology of 20th Century Native American Poetry* (San Francisco: HarperCollins, 1988), xx. For a helpful discussion on methods of reading Native American poetry that do justice to the writers and texts, see Susan Brill, "Discovering the Order and Structure of Things: A Conversive Approach to Contemporary Navajo Poetry," *Studies in American Indian Literatures* 7 (1995): 51–70.

5.   Leslie Marmon Silko, *Laguna Woman: Poems by Leslie Silko* (Greenfield Center, N.Y.: Greenfield Review Press, 1974); hereafter cited parenthetically in text.

6.   For a helpful discussion of notions of time and space in Native American cultures, see Vine Deloria Jr.'s *God is Red: A Native View of Religion* (Boulder, Colo.: Fulcrum, 1994).

Chapter Three

1.   Leslie Marmon Silko, *Ceremony* (New York: Viking, 1977), 1; hereafter cited parenthetically in text.

2.   I call these verse sections of the novel poems simply because they are set in poetic form. Silko imagines these sections being spoken aloud during the reading. In an interview Kim Barnes asked Silko about the strategy behind the use of form.

KB: Do you write what you think to be prose poems? You seem to be bucking traditional form, and we've already talked about how you want it to look on a page to give the sense of storytellers. Are you working on anything new or unique in doing this type of writing? I mean, this blurring between verse and prose. And why, as in *Ceremony,* where it will break in?

LS: Well, in *Ceremony* the breaks would be the parts that ideally you would hear rather than read. As far as what I'm doing with the blurring of the two, Virgil and the old dudes, the old cats back in the old days, or the Greeks, they didn't worry so much it seems to me, although I'm sure some of the genre definitions and stuff came out of that period of time. In some ways, I feel that it's more valid to have a checklist or a discussion of what constitutes tragedy or comedy than what constitutes poetry or prose. I don't decide I'll take a stance. For my purposes, it's just useless, it's stupid, it doesn't interest me at all. What I'm interested in is getting a feeling or an idea that's part of the story. Getting the story across. And I'm really not particular how it's done. The important thing is that it goes across in a way that I want it to go. I don't waste my time on it. But if other people want to worry over whether what they've just written is a poem or prose poem, if they want to worry about that or if literary critics want to worry about that, I don't like to tell people what they should spend their time on. I don't spend my time like that. (Barnes, 59)

3. Pueblos believe in the existence of four worlds previous to this one. This fifth world was arrived at after they went through the other four, which are located inside the earth. Antelope and Badger helped to open the *sipapu*, or emergence place into the fifth world, thus the Antelope and Badger clans are particularly honored. See Silko's *Yellow Woman and A Beauty of the Spirit*, Elsie Clews Parsons, *Pueblo Indian Religion* (Chicago: University of Chicago Press, 1939), and Alfonse Ortiz, *New Perspectives on the Pueblos* (Albuquerque, N.Mex.: University of New Mexico Press, 1972) for helpful information on Pueblo mythology and religion.

4. James Ruppert remarks: "If the reader follows and understands the fusion of the story and reality, he too sees how all the stories merge into the story that is being told. He has effectively been educated into the unity that strengthens Tayo and brings back the rain and its blessings. Also, he has been introduced into the experience of the oral tradition. The perceptive reader, too, has the ear for the story, the eye for the pattern, and is encouraged to see the world as one large swirling sand painting." "The Reader's Lessons in Ceremony," *Arizona Quarterly* 44 (1988): 84.

5. Michael Hobbs, "Living In-Between: Tayo as Radical Reader in Leslie Marmon Silko's *Ceremony*," *Western American Literature* 28 (1994): 301–12.

6. Leon is an example of this phenomenon in "Tony's Story" in *Storyteller*.

7. The twins play a prominent role in much of Native American mythology from the Mayans to the woodland tribes. They appear most frequently, however, in southwestern Native American mythology and particularly in Pueblo mythology. See Åke Hultkrantz, *The Religions of the American Indians*, trans. Monica Setterwall (Berkeley: University of California Press, 1967), 38–42, and Charles F. Lummis, *Pueblo Indian Folk-Stories* (Lincoln: University of Nebraska Press, 1992).

8. See Silko's poem "Deer Song" in *Storyteller* and her essay "Interior and Exterior Landscapes" in *Yellow Woman and A Beauty of the Spirit* for discussions on the role of deer in Laguna mythology.

9. The alcoholic Indian is both a stereotype in popular culture from at least the seventeenth century and a trope in much Native American fiction. The trope is used in a different manner in N. Scott Momaday's *House Made of Dawn* (New York: Harper & Row, 1968), James Welch's *Winter in the Blood* (New York: Penguin, 1974), and Aaron Yava's collection of drawings, for which Silko wrote the introduction, *Border Towns of the Navajo Nation* (Alamo, Calif.: Holmganger Press, 1975). For a discussion of the trope, see Nicholas O. Warner, "Images of Drinking in 'Woman Singing,' *Ceremony*, and *House Made of Dawn*," *MELUS: The*

Journal of the Society for the Study of the Multi-Ethnic Literature of the United States, 11 (1984): 15–30. Michael Dorris has also written a widely read autobiographical and sociological account of alcohol consumption among Native Americans titled *The Broken Cord* (New York: HarperCollins, 1989).

10.   Robert M. Nelson, *Place and Vision: The Function of Landscape in Native American Fiction* (New York: Peter Lang, 1993), 12–13.

11.   Paula Gunn Allen, *The Sacred Hoop: Recovering the Feminine in American Indian Traditions* (Boston: Beacon Press, 1986), 118; hereafter cited in text as Allen.

Chapter Four

1.   Leslie Marmon Silko, *Storyteller* (New York: Viking, 1981); hereafter cited parenthetically in text.

2.   Short stories that are not here are "Bravura" and "from Humaweepi, the Warrior Priest." These stories may be found in Kenneth Rosen, ed., *The Man to Send Rain Clouds: Contemporary Stories by American Indians* (New York: Viking, 1974). "Gallup, Indian Capital of the World" was eventually worked into *Ceremony.*

3.   Donna Perry, "Leslie Marmon Silko," *Backtalk: Women Writers Speak Out,* ed. Donna Perry (New Brunswick: Rutgers University Press, 1992), 323; hereafter cited in text as Perry.

4.   See Elsie Clews Parsons, *Tewa Tales* (New York: American Folk-Lore Society, 1926); Franz Boas, *Keresan Texts,* Anthropological Papers of the American Museum of Natural History (New York: The Trustees, 1928) 8, part 1; hereafter cited in text as Boas; John Gunn, *Schat-chen: History, Tradition, and Narratives of the Queres Indians of Laguna and Acoma* (Albuquerque, N.Mex.: Albright and Andersen, 1917); and Charles F. Lummis, *Pueblo Indian Folk-Stories* (Lincoln: University of Nebraska Press, 1992).

5.   The story behind this ritual is not unique to the Laguna or even the Pueblos. Many Native American tribes understand the hunt as a sacred ritual involving the willing sacrifice of the deer. See Sam Gill, *Native American Religions: An Introduction* (Belmont, Calif.: Wadsworth, 1982) and Joseph Epes Brown, *The Spiritual Legacy of the American Indian* (New York: Crossroad, 1982).

6.   The Marmons were Presbyterian missionaries and surveyors who represented the final conquest of Laguna by their intermarriage and political and religious successes. See Per Seyersted, *Leslie Marmon Silko,* Western Writers Series (Boise: Boise State University, 1980) and A. LaVonne Ruoff, "Ritual and Renewal: Keres Traditions in the Short Fiction of Leslie Silko," *MELUS: The Journal of the Society for the Study of the Multi-Ethnic Literature of the United States* 5 (1978): 2–17; hereafter cited in text as Ruoff.

7.   Bernard A. Hirsch, " 'The telling which continues': Oral Tradition and the Written Word in Leslie Marmon Silko's *Storyteller,*" *American Indian Quarterly* 12 (1988): 3; hereafter cited in text as Hirsch.

8.   Allen uses a slightly different spelling of the Keresan word.

9. The story first appeared in *Redbook*.

10. Lawrence J. Evers, "The Killing of a New Mexican State Trooper: Ways of Telling a Historical Event," *Critical Essays on American Literature*, ed. Andrew Wiget (Boston: Hall, 1985): 247, 255.

11. For an excellent analysis of witchcraft in the southwestern tribes, see Marc Simmons, *Witchcraft in the Southwest: Spanish and Indian Supernaturalism on the Rio Grande* (Lincoln: University of Nebraska Press, 1974).

12. See Vine Deloria Jr., *Custer Died for Your Sins* (Norman, Okla.: University of Oklahoma Press, 1988): "It has always been a great disappointment to Indian people that the humorous side of Indian life has not been mentioned by professed experts on Indian Affairs" (146).

13. Jennifer Browdy de Hernandez, "Laughing, Crying, Surviving: The Pragmatic Politics of Leslie Marmon Silko's *Storyteller*," *A/B: Auto/Biography Studies* 9 (1994): 39.

Chapter Five

1. Ann Wright, ed., *The Delicacy and Strength of Lace: Letters Between Leslie Marmon Silko and James Wright* (St. Paul, Minn.: Graywolf Press, 1986).

2. *Sacred Water* (Tucson: Flood Plain Press, 1993); hereafter cited parenthetically in text.

3. Lagunas believe that when they die, they go on to a place called Cliff House, which is simply "over there." See *Yellow Woman and A Beauty of the Spirit* for discussions of Cliff House.

4. This reciprocity is at the center of the short story "The Man to Send Rain Clouds."

5. There is a copy of one of these early volumes archived in special collections at the University of Arizona library.

6. Walter J. Ong, *Orality and Literacy: The Technologizing of the Word* (New York: Methuen, 1982), and Marshall McLuhan, *The Gutenberg Galaxy* (Toronto: University of Toronto Press, 1962).

7. See Mircea Eliade, *Patterns in Comparative Religion*, trans. Rosemary Sheed (New York: Meridian Books, 1963).

Chapter Six

1. Leslie Marmon Silko, *Almanac of the Dead* (New York: Simon & Schuster, 1991); hereafter cited parenthetically in text.

2. A good example of a Mayan text that functions as almanac, creation myth, ritual script, and visual text is the *Popol Vuh*. See Dennis Tedlock, trans., *Popol Vuh* (New York: Simon & Schuster, 1985).

3. For background information on the ancient Mesoamerican almanacs and on the novel in general, readers are referred to *Yellow Woman and A Beauty of the Spirit*, especially pages 124–65.

4. A cacique is a local chief. This story has similarities to Pueblo emergence myths that involve the cacique and the war twins finding their way out

of the *sipapu*. See Hamilton Tyler, *Pueblo Gods and Myths* (Norman: University of Oklahoma Press, 1964), 106; he remarks: "The meaning of the emergence myths thus seems to be twofold: it explains how men came upon the surface of the earth and how they rose out of chaos" (107).

 5. For an excellent analysis of the role uranium mining plays in Pueblo culture, see Helen Jaskoski, and G. Lynn Nelson (reply), "Thinking Woman's Children and the Bomb," *Explorations in Ethnic Studies: The Journal of the National Association for Ethnic Studies* 13 (1990): 1–24.

 6. Janet St. Clair, "Uneasy Ethnocentrism: Recent Works of Allen, Silko, and Hogan," *Studies in American Indian Literatures: The Journal of the Association for the Study of American Indian Literatures* 6 (1994): 93 hereafter cited in text as St. Clair.

 7. This item is autobiographical as well. Silko was having these sorts of dreams herself during the writing of *Almanac of the Dead:* "I began to have vivid dreams. Early one morning, I dreamed U.S. Army helicopters were flying out of the south. I saw them flying low over saguaro cactus forests with their doors wide open. They flew low enough in my dream that I could look inside the helicopter doors. I saw dead and wounded U.S. soldiers. I knew they had died in a war in Mexico, and that Tucson has become like Saigon in the days of the Vietnam War" (*YWBS*, 139).

 8. Vine Deloria Jr., *God Is Red: A Native View of Religion* (Golden, Colo.: Fulcrum, 1994), 276.

 9. For examples of such literature, see Julian Barnes, *A History of the World in 10 1/2 Chapters* (New York: Vintage, 1989), Margaret Atwood, *The Handmaid's Tale* (Boston: Houghton Mifflin Co., 1986), and Don DeLillo, *White Noise* (New York: Penguin, 1984). There are, of course, any number of films that detail the apocalyptic mood of American culture in the late twentieth century (*Apocalypse Now* is probably the most obvious of these).

Chapter Seven

 1. *Yellow Woman and A Beauty of the Spirit* (New York: Simon & Schuster, 1996); hereafter cited parenthetically in text.

 2. Silko defines this term in a footnote as the last generation or two that would include her great-grandmother because the worldview of that generation was uniquely Pueblo.

 3. There is a fundamental split in Western mythology between the essential and the excessive that expresses itself in a number of ways, from the mind-body problem to the notions of waste. Those who carried this mythology to the North American continent saw the "wilderness" and its inhabitants (including indigenous peoples) as excess and inessential.

Chapter Eight

 1. Per Seyersted, *Leslie Marmon Silko,* Western Writers Series (Boise: Boise State University, 1980), 5.

2. Paula Gunn Allen, "Special Problems in Teaching Leslie Marmon Silko's Ceremony," *American Indian Quarterly: A Journal of Anthropology, History and Literature* 14 (1990): 383.

3. Leslie Marmon Silko, "Here's an Odd Artifact for the Fairy-Tale Shelf," *Studies in American Indian Literatures: The Journal of the Association for the Study of American Indian Literatures* 10 (1986): 179. For an excellent analysis of the review, see Susan Perez Castillo, "Postmodernism, Native American Literature and the Real: The Silko-Erdrich Controversy," *Massachusetts Review: A Quarterly of Literature, the Arts and Public Affairs* 32 (1991): 285–94.

4. Quoted in Reyes García, "Senses of Place in *Ceremony*," *MELUS: The Journal of the Society for the Study of the Multi-Ethnic Literature of the United States* 10 (1983): 37–48.

Selected Bibliography

Primary Sources

Published Works

Laguna Woman: Poems by Leslie Silko. Greenfield Center, N.Y.: Greenfield Review Press, 1974.
Ceremony. New York: Viking, 1977.
Storyteller. New York: Viking, 1981.
The Delicacy and Strength of Lace: Letters Between Leslie Marmon Silko and James Wright, ed. Ann Wright. St. Paul, Minn.: Graywolf Press, 1986.
Almanac of the Dead. New York: Simon & Schuster, 1991.
Sacred Water: Narratives and Pictures. Tucson, Ariz.: Flood Plain Press, 1993.
Yellow Woman and a Beauty of the Spirit: Essays on Native American Life Today. New York: Simon & Schuster, 1996.
Garden in the Dunes. New York: Simon & Schuster, forthcoming.

Unpublished or Miscellaneous Materials

"Aaron Yava." *Yardbird Reader* 3 (1974): 98–103.
"Bravura." *The Man to Send Rain Clouds: Contemporary Stories by American Indians,* ed. Kenneth Rosen. New York: Viking, 1974. 149–54.
"From Humaweepi, the Warrior Priest." *The Man to Send Rain Clouds: Contemporary Stories by American Indians,* ed. Kenneth Rosen. New York: Viking, 1974. 161–68.
A Conversation with Leslie Marmon Silko. Prod. Lawrence J. Evers and Dennis W. Carr. Videotape. 1975.
"An Old-Time Indian Attack Conducted in Two Parts." *Yardbird Reader* 5 (1976): 77–84.
The Laguna Regulars and Geronimo. Akwesasne Notes. Audiotape. 1977.
Estoyehmuut and the Kunideeyah (Arrowboy and the Destroyers), with Dennis W. Carr. Film. 1980.
Running on the Edge of the Rainbow: Laguna Stories and Poems. Clearwater. Words and Place Videocassette Series. New York, 1982.
Ingram, Helen M., Lawrence A. Scaff, and Leslie Marmon Silko. "Replacing Confusion with Equity: Alternatives for Water Policy in the Colorado River Basin." *New Courses for the Colorado River: Major Issues for the Next Century,* ed. Gary D. Weatherford and F. Lee Brown. Albuquerque, N.Mex.: University of New Mexico Press, 1984. 177–99.
"Here's an Odd Artifact for the Fairy-Tale Shelf." *Impact/Albuquerque Journal* 8 (October 1986): 10–11.
Leslie Marmon Silko. University of Missouri. Audiotape. 1991.

Secondary Sources

Books and Parts of Books

GENERAL

Barnes, Kim. "A Leslie Marmon Silko Interview." *Leslie Marmon Silko, "Yellow Woman,"* ed. Melody Graulich. New Brunswick, N.J.: Rutgers University Press, 1993. Pages 47–65 of *Women Writers: Texts and Contexts*. An especially good interview because of its length and breadth in a collection of essays devoted to the Yellow Woman theme.

Boas, Franz. *Keresan Texts*. Anthropological Papers of the American Museum of Natural History. New York: The Trustees, 1928. An ethnographic collection of tales from the Keresan-speaking pueblos, including Laguna.

Fisher, Dexter. "Stories and Their Tellers: A Conversation with Leslie Marmon Silko." *The Third Woman: Minority Women Writers of the United States,* ed. Dexter Fisher. Boston: Houghton Mifflin Co., 1980. 18–23. A short but instructive interview that reveals some of the problems in Alaska, what Silko reads (Milton and Shakespeare), and her thoughts on literary criticism.

Jahner, Elaine. "The Novel and Oral Tradition: An Interview with Leslie Marmon Silko." *Book Forum: An International Transdisciplinary Quarterly* 5 (1981): 383–88. An essay that reflects upon an interview and focuses mainly upon *Ceremony*.

Perry, Donna. "Leslie Marmon Silko." *Backtalk: Women Writers Speak Out,* ed. Donna Perry. New Brunswick: Rutgers University Press, 1992. 313–40. An excellent interview that covers everything from Silko's childhood to *Almanac of the Dead*.

Seyersted, Per. *Leslie Marmon Silko*. Boise: Boise State University, 1980. A short but useful pamphlet (50 pages) on Silko's early work.

Silko, Leslie Marmon, and Laura Coltelli. "Leslie Marmon Silko." *Winged Words: American Indian Writers Speak,* ed. Laura Coltelli. Lincoln: University of Nebraska Press, 1990. 134–53. A broad and useful discussion of Silko's approach to writing among other things.

CEREMONY

Allen, Paula Gunn. *The Sacred Hoop: Recovering the Feminine in American Indian Traditions*. Boston: Beacon Press, 1986. A wide-ranging collection of essays from a Laguna writer and critic that mentions Silko often.

Harvey, Valerie. "Navajo Sandpainting in *Ceremony*." *Critical Perspectives on Native American Fiction,* ed. Richard F. Fleck. Washington, D.C.: Three Continents Press, 1993. 256–59. A short but important analysis of the actual ceremony.

Larson, Charles R. *American Indian Fiction*. Albuquerque, N.Mex.: University of New Mexico Press, 1978. An introduction to the field that contains a useful section on *Ceremony*.

Lincoln, Kenneth. *Native American Renaissance*. Berkeley: University of California Press, 1983. An essential guide to Native American literature in general with a superb reading of *Ceremony* that is reflective of Laguna life and landscape.

Nelson, Robert M. *Place and Vision: The Function of Landscape in Native American Fiction.* New York: Peter Lang, 1993. A superb and detailed analysis of the function of landscape in *Ceremony,* using the specifics of place and orientation.

Owens, Louis. *Other Destinies: Understanding the American Indian Novel.* Norman, Okla.: University of Oklahoma Press, 1992 vol. 3. Another fine introduction to Native American literature that interprets *Ceremony* as a search for identity.

Velie, Alan R. *Four American Indian Literary Masters: N. Scott Momaday, James Welch, Leslie Marmon Silko, and Gerald Vizenor.* Norman: University of Oklahoma Press, 1982. Offers an interpretation of *Ceremony* as a grail story.

STORYTELLER

Evers, Lawrence J. "The Killing of a New Mexican State Trooper: Ways of Telling an Historical Event." *Critical Essays on American Literature,* ed. Andrew Wiget. Boston: Hall, 1985. 246–61. Provides the details of the true story behind "Tony's Story" and offers an interesting comparison between Silko's story and a similar one by Simon Ortiz.

Graulich, Melody, ed. *Leslie Marmon Silko, "Yellow Woman."* New Brunswick, N.J.: Rutgers University Press, 1993. Essential reading on the Yellow Woman theme that includes some of the best essays written on *Storyteller.*

Krupat, Arnold. "The Dialogic of Silko's *Storyteller.*" *Narrative Chance: Postmodern Discourse on Native American Indian Literatures,* ed. Gerald Vizenor. Albuquerque: University of New Mexico Press, 1989. 55–68. Interprets the structure of *Storyteller* through the dialogical theory of Mikhail Bakhtin and with an understanding of the nature of autobiography.

Sands, Kathleen Mullen. "Indian Women's Personal Narrative: Voices Past and Present." *American Women's Autobiography: Fea(s)ts of Memory,* ed. Margo Culley. Madison: University of Wisconsin Press, 1992. 268–94. Discusses *Storyteller* in the context of women's autobiography.

Wong, Hertha D. "Contemporary Innovations of Oral Traditions: N. Scott Momaday and Leslie Marmon Silko." *Sending My Heart Back across the Years,* ed. Hertha D. Wong. New York: Oxford University Press, 1992. 153–99. A useful survey of the use of the oral traditions of several Native American novelists including Silko.

Articles

GENERAL

Evers, Lawrence J., and Dennis W. Carr. "A Conversation with Leslie Marmon Silko." *Sun Tracks: An American Indian Literary Magazine* 3 (1976): 28–33. An early interview where Silko discusses growing up in Laguna and writing *Ceremony.*

Perez Castillo, Susan. "Postmodernism, Native American Literature and the Real: The Silko-Erdrich Controversy." *Massachusetts Review: A Quarterly of Literature, the Arts and Public Affairs* 32 (1991): 285–94. Explores Silko's motivations for her negative review of Louise Erdrich's *Beet Queen*.

Seyersted, Per. "Two Interviews with Leslie Marmon Silko." *American Studies in Scandinavia* 13 (1981): 17–33. A discussion of many things including the politics of literature and literary criticism.

CEREMONY

Allen, Paula Gunn. "Special Problems in Teaching Leslie Marmon Silko's *Ceremony*." *American Indian Quarterly: A Journal of Anthropology, History and Literature* 14 (1990): 379–86. A fellow Laguna writer criticizes Silko's public telling of a clan story.

Antell, Judith A. "Momaday, Welch, and Silko: Expressing the Feminine Principle through Male Alienation." *American Indian Quarterly* 12 (1988): 213–20. Explores the dynamics of gender in relation to other Native American novelists.

Benediktsson, Thomas E. "The Reawakening of the Gods: Realism and the Supernatural in Silko and Hulme." *Critique: Studies in Contemporary Fiction* 33 (1992): 121–31. Focuses on the disruptive narrative line in the novel.

Berner, Robert L. "Trying to Be Round: Three American Indian Novels." *World Literature Today: A Literary Quarterly of the University of Oklahoma* 58 (1984): 341–44. Short but interesting comparison of Momaday, Welch, and Silko.

Blumenthal, Susan. "Spotted Cattle and Deer: Spirit Guides and Symbols of Endurance and Healing in *Ceremony*." *American Indian Quarterly* 14 (1990): 367–77. One of the few essays that explores the function of animals in the novel.

García, Reyes. "Senses of Place in *Ceremony*." *MELUS: The Journal of the Society for the Study of the Multi-Ethnic Literature of the United States* 10 (1983): 37–48. A study of the sense of place embodied by Tayo at the end of the ceremony.

Hobbs, Michael. "Living In-Between: Tayo as Radical Reader in Leslie Marmon Silko's *Ceremony*." *Western American Literature* 28 (1994): 301–12. A superb analysis of the problem of interpretation that Tayo faces.

Hoilman, Dennis. " 'A World Made of Stories': An Interpretation of Leslie Silko's *Ceremony*." *South Dakota Review* 17 (1979): 54–66. An analysis of the collapse of white distinctions between narrative and performance.

Jaskoski, Helen, and G. Lynn Nelson (reply). "Thinking Woman's Children and the Bomb." *Explorations in Ethnic Studies: The Journal of the National Association for Ethnic Studies* 13 (1990): 1–24. A discussion of the role of nuclear technology in the lives of the Pueblo people and Silko's response to the juxtaposition of an ancient culture with the technology that threatens to obliterate all cultures.

Manley, Kathleen. "Leslie Marmon Silko's Use of Color in *Ceremony*." *Southern Folklore* 46 (1989): 133–46. Draws upon anthropology and Laguna mythology to explore the meanings of various colors in particular settings.

Purdy, John. "The Transformation: Tayo's Genealogy in *Ceremony*." *Studies in American Indian Literature: The Journal of the Association for the Study of American Indian Literature* 10 (1986): 121–33. Discusses possible sources for Tayo's character in older Laguna narratives.

Rainwater, Catherine. "The Semiotics of Dwelling in Leslie Marmon Silko's *Ceremony*." *The American Journal of Semiotics* 9 (1992): 219–40. A semiotic approach to interpreting Tayo's "crisis of dwelling."

Ruppert, James. "Dialogism and Mediation in Leslie Silko's *Ceremony*." *Explicator* 51 (1993): 129–34. Interprets the novel from the perspective of Mikhail Bakhtin's theory of dialogism.

———. "The Reader's Lessons in *Ceremony*." *Arizona Quarterly* 44 (1988): 78–85. Explores the reader's relationship to Tayo through the mediation of the text.

Sands, Kathleen M. "A Special Symposium Issue on Leslie Marmon Silko's *Ceremony*." *American Indian Quarterly: A Journal of Anthropology, History and Literature* 5 (1979): 1–5. An entire volume of *AIQ* that contains important essays on the novel just after it was published.

St. Andrews, B. A. "Healing the Witchery: Medicine in Silko's *Ceremony*." *Arizona Quarterly* 44 (1988): 86–94. A short but useful discussion of conflicting notions of medicine.

Swan, Edith E.. "Feminine Perspectives at Laguna Pueblo: Silko's *Ceremony*." *Tulsa Studies in Women's Literature* 11 (1992): 309–27. An essay that builds upon Allen's work on the importance of the feminine in the novel.

———. "Healing via the Sunwise Cycle in Silko's *Ceremony*." *American Indian Quarterly* 12 (1988): 313–28. Carefully detailed reading of the geography and orientation of Tayo's cure.

———. "Laguna Prototypes of Manhood in *Ceremony*." *MELUS: The Journal of the Society for the Study of the Multi-Ethnic Literature of the United States* 17 (1991): 39–61. Analyzes the hunter/warrior motif in relation to Yellow Woman.

———. "Laguna Symbolic Geography and Silko's *Ceremony*." *American Indian Quarterly* 12 (1988): 229–49. Further exploration of landscape features and directions in relation to color.

Truesdale, C. W. "Tradition and *Ceremony*: Leslie Marmon Silko as an American Novelist." *North Dakota Quarterly* 59 (1991): 200–28. Places the themes of the novel in relation to similar themes in other writers.

STORYTELLER

Browdy de Hernandez, Jennifer. "Laughing, Crying, Surviving: The Pragmatic Politics of Leslie Marmon Silko's *Storyteller*." *A/B: Auto/Biography Studies* 9 (1994). An excellent analysis of both the whole and the parts of *Storyteller*.

Danielson, Linda L. "*Storyteller:* Grandmother Spider's Web." *Journal of the Southwest* 30 (1988): 325–55. Explores the relationship between women and narrative.

Hirsch, Bernard A. " 'The telling Which Continues': Oral Tradition and the Written Word in Leslie Marmon Silko's *Storyteller.*" *American Indian Quarterly* 12 (1988): 1–26. Excellent analysis of the use of form and its effects upon the reader. Pays careful attention to the whole as well as the parts.

Krumholz, Linda J. " 'To Understand This World Differently': Reading and Subversion in Leslie Marmon Silko's *Storyteller.*" *Ariel: A Review of International English Literature* 25 (1994): 89–113. Explores the political dimension of the book by suggesting that it creates a "double consciousness" in nonnative readers.

Langen, Toby C. S. "*Storyteller* as Hopi Basket." *Studies in American Indian Literatures: The Journal of the Association for the Study of American Indian Literatures* 5 (1993): 7–24. Discusses the book in terms of its thematic clusters and offers close readings of some of Silko's interludes.

Lucero, Ambrose. "For the People: Leslie Silko's *Storyteller.*" *Minority Voices: An Interdisciplinary Journal of Literature and the Arts* 5 (1981): 1–10. Argues that Silko encompasses ethnic differences without losing ethnic identity in her storytelling.

Nelson, Robert M. "He Said/She Said: Writing Oral Tradition in John Gunn's 'Ko-pot Ka-nat' and Leslie Silko's *Storyteller.*" *Studies in American Indian Literatures: The Journal of the Association for the Study of American Indian Literatures* 5 (1993): 31–50. Analyzes the possible sources for Silko's characters from the oral tradition and compares their respective functions.

Ruppert, Jim. "Story Telling: The Fiction of Leslie Silko." *The Journal of Ethnic Studies* 9 (1981): 53–58. A discussion of the creation of a story world that supersedes the world of objective reality.

Schubnell, Matthias. "Frozen Suns and Angry Bears: An Interpretation of Leslie Silko's *Storyteller.*" *European Review of Native American Studies* 1 (1987): 21–25. An ecological and apocalyptic reading of the short story.

ALMANAC OF THE DEAD

Holland, Sharon P. " 'If You Know I Have a History, You Will Respect Me': A Perspective on Afro-Native American Literature." *Callaloo: A Journal of African-American and African Arts and Letters* 17 (1994): 334–50. Explores the concept of Afro-Native subjectivity in relation to American ideology.

Norden, Christopher. "Ecological Restoration as Post-Colonial Ritual of Community in Three Native American Novels." *Studies in American Indian Literatures: The Journal of the Association for the Study of American Indian Literatures* 6 (1994): 94–106. Discusses the role of alienation in Native American fiction and the opportunities for renewal through intercultural ritual and dialogue.

St. Clair, Janet. "Uneasy Ethnocentrism: Recent Works of Allen, Silko, and Hogan." *Studies in American Indian Literatures: The Journal of the Association for the Study of American Indian Literatures* 6 (1994): 82–98. A very helpful examination of the double play of ethnocentrism and "a transcendent feminist philosophical solution" to the problems of "America" and its discontents.

Index

The Author

Gregory Salyer is assistant professor of humanities at Huntingdon College in Montgomery, Alabama, where he directs the Liberal Arts Symposium, an interdisciplinary sequence in the core curriculum. He teaches courses in literature, philosophy, and religion, including Native American literature and religion. He received his Ph.D. from Emory University's Graduate Institute of the Liberal Arts and later served as assistant director of the Institute. He is coeditor with Robert Detweiler of *Literature and Theology at Century's End* (Scholars Press, 1995). He is the North American editor for *Literature and Theology: An International Journal of Theory, Criticism, and Culture*. In addition, he has published articles in books and journals on Native American literature, postmodernism, the Bible, and mythology.

The Editor

Frank Day is a professor of English and head of the English Department at Clemson University. He is the author of *Sir William Empson: An Annotated Bibliography* (1984) and *Arthur Koestler: A Guide to Research* (1985). He was a Fulbright lecturer in American literature in Romania (1980–1981) and in Bangladesh (1986–1987).

ORLAND PARK
PUBLIC LIBRARY
A Natural Connection

**14921 Ravinia Avenue
Orland Park, IL 60462**

**708-428-5100
orlandparklibrary.org**